TECHNICAL REPORT

Integrated Planning for the Air Force Senior Leader Workforce

Background and Methods

Albert A. Robbert, Stephen M. Drezner,
John Boon, Larry Hanser, Craig Moore,
Lynn Scott, Herbert J. Shukiar

Prepared for the United States Air Force

RAND PROJECT AIR FORCE

The research reported here was sponsored by the United States Air Force under Contract F49642-01-C-0003. Further information may be obtained from the Strategic Planning Division, Directorate of Plans, Hq USAF.

Library of Congress Cataloging-in-Publication Data

Integrated planning for the Air Force senior leader workforce : background and methods / Albert A. Robbert ... [et al.].
    p. cm.
    "TR-175."
    Includes bibliographical references.
    ISBN 0-8330-3663-7 (pbk.)
    1. Generals—Selection and appointment—United States. 2. Generals—Training of—United States. 3. United States. Air Force—Selection and appointment. 4. United States. Air Force—Officers—Training of. I. Robbert, Albert A., 1944–

UG793.I54 2005
358.4'1331—dc22

                                                                                    2004018246

The RAND Corporation is a nonprofit research organization providing objective analysis and effective solutions that address the challenges facing the public and private sectors around the world. RAND's publications do not necessarily reflect the opinions of its research clients and sponsors.

RAND® is a registered trademark.

Published 2005 by the RAND Corporation
1776 Main Street, P.O. Box 2138, Santa Monica, CA 90407-2138
1200 South Hayes Street, Arlington, VA 22202-5050
201 North Craig Street, Suite 202, Pittsburgh, PA 15213-1516
RAND URL: http://www.rand.org/
To order RAND documents or to obtain additional information, contact
Distribution Services: Telephone: (310) 451-7002;
Fax: (310) 451-6915; Email: order@rand.org

Preface

Organizations such as the United States Air Force, which encompass a wide variety of operational, technical, and business-oriented activities, are complex. And the task of ensuring the continued availability of individuals having the competencies required to lead those activities effectively is also complex, especially in an organization that largely selects leaders from within its own ranks. This study, conducted in the Manpower, Personnel, and Training Program of RAND Project AIR FORCE, examined

- Competency requirements for Air Force senior leader positions, including both general officer (GO) and Senior Executive Service (SES) positions.

- Optimal competency mixes in the inventory of senior leaders, recognizing that competency requirements for individual positions cannot be met perfectly in a closed personnel system.

- Flexibility in the boundary between GO and SES utilization in order to better meet organizational needs and enhance career development.

This work was chartered in 1998 by Gen Michael E. Ryan, then Chief of Staff of the United States Air Force, who saw it as a way to better understand how to develop senior personnel with both the operational knowledge and the technical skills needed to lead the future Air Force. The research described here was conducted within RAND Project AIR FORCE in partnership with the Air Force General Officer Matters Office (AFGOMO) and its successor, the Air Force Senior Leader Management Office (AFSLMO). Current and future efforts continue to develop this body of research.

The research sponsor considers many of this study's findings to be sensitive, so this report generally does not present detailed findings. However, since the methods that were developed and used in the study are likely to be of interest to other organizations seeking to establish or enhance competency-based, requirements-driven leadership development programs, this report describes those methods, providing sufficient background to place them in context. The primary audience for this report consists of human resource and line managers interested in applying similar methods in their own organizations.

RAND Project AIR FORCE

RAND Project AIR FORCE (PAF), a division of the RAND Corporation, is the U.S. Air Force's federally funded research and development center for studies and analyses. PAF provides the Air Force with independent analyses of policy alternatives affecting the development, employment, combat readiness, and support of current and future aerospace forces. Research is performed in four programs: Aerospace Force Development; Manpower, Personnel, and Training; Resource Management; and Strategy and Doctrine.

Additional information about PAF is available on the RAND Web site, at http://www.rand.org/paf.

Contents

Figures

Tables

Summary

As Chief of Staff of the Air Force in 1998, Gen Michael E. Ryan observed a mismatch between the qualifications of Air Force general officers (GOs) and some of the jobs they needed to fill. Finding too few candidates with backgrounds appropriate for filling senior warfighting positions and many GOs with backgrounds too specialized to be very useful at higher grades, he asked RAND Project AIR FORCE (PAF), a division of the RAND Corporation, to help improve the Air Force's GO development approach. Through an initial position-level analysis, PAF found that selectivity could be increased and utilization improved if GOs, including those who came from operational backgrounds, had broader experience. Based on these findings, the senior leadership of the Air Force chartered PAF and the Air Force General Officer Matters Office (AFGOMO) to undertake a more detailed study. As this study unfolded, PAF and its Air Force sponsors recognized that a significant part of the Air Force senior leadership need is supplied by members of the Senior Executive Service (SES). Accordingly, the study was expanded to include that segment of the senior leader force.[1]

To execute this study, PAF and the Air Force

- Identified required competencies for each GO and SES position. (See pages 7–16.)

- Identified the ideal mix of competencies among annual cohorts promoted into the GO and SES ranks using a model of the flow of individuals through GO grades and career progression tiers within the SES. (See pages 17–26.)

- Constructed templates to guide the development of competitive middle-grade officers and civil servants based on the competency distributions within these entry cohorts. (See page 26.)

- Examined the boundary between GO and SES utilization to find new flexibilities in meeting senior leader needs. (See pages 27–32.)

---

[1] As an eventual consequence of this decision, the Air Force Senior Executive Matters Office (AFSEMO), which managed the SES workforce, merged with AFGOMO in 2002 to form the Air Force Senior Leader Management Office (AFSLMO).

- Employed the flow model and other, related analyses to help the Air Force improve the identification and GO/SES mix of the set of senior leader positions it intends to fill (referred to as the *objective force*). (See pages 33–39.)

- Constructed a decision support system (DSS) prototype to help the Air Force employ competency information in GO assignment actions. (See pages 41–45.)

As PAF worked through these steps, a framework for organizing competency requirements emerged. Most jobs were found to have a *primary occupational competency:* prior experience gained in a specific operational/functional area (e.g., fighter pilot) or a "bin" containing a number of such areas that is critical to success in the position. Many positions also required a *secondary occupational competency:* prior experience in a second operational/functional area or bin. Primary and secondary occupational competencies can be considered "provider-level" skills—that is, the individual is expected to be able to manage the provision of services generated in the function. Additionally, all jobs require multiple areas of *functional familiarity,* which is defined as the ability to be an informed consumer of services generated by other functions. Finally, all jobs require an array of *cross-functional competencies:* leadership skills, management skills, and other competencies that are common across positions in many operational/functional areas.

Methods employed in the study included

- Surveys of incumbents, initially using paper-and-pencil instruments, and later using Web-based or email-based electronic versions. (See pages 8–9.)

- Review and synthesis of survey results by PAF and relatively senior (lieutenant general or SES equivalent) panels of knowledgeable Air Force representatives. (See pages 9–10.)

- Linear programming modeling to optimize objective force configurations (see pages 38–39) and the flow of individuals through positions. (See pages 18–24.)

- Construction and application of rules to determine military or civilian essentiality of senior leader positions. (See pages 30–31.)

- Statistical regression analysis to quantify the relative needs for senior leaders within Air Force organizations. (See pages 35–38.)

- Systematic software development practices to construct a prototype DSS. (See pages 41–45.)

The study's major findings are as follows:

- Most positions require a secondary competency, giving rise to the need for *simultaneous* multifunctionality: the incumbent needs both primary and secondary competencies to enhance his/her success in a given position. (See page 17.)

- Within the set of jobs sharing a common primary occupational competency, grade requirements often do not form a neat career progression pyramid: with expected promotion patterns, individuals cannot progress from grade to grade (GO) or tier to tier (SES) within the same primary occupational competency. Accordingly, individuals must shift among primary occupational pyramids as they rise through the grades or tiers, giving rise to the need for *serial* multifunctionality. (See pages 17–19.)

- Recent cohorts of individuals selected for promotion to brigadier general approximately matched the ideal distribution of primary occupational competencies but exhibited the required multifunctionality to only a very limited degree. To provide the needed competencies in the future, deliberate efforts must be made to broaden competitive middle-grade officers. (See pages 25–26.)

- While most positions have characteristics that make them suitable only for GO incumbents in some cases and SES incumbents in others, a sizable minority of positions can be filled "flexibly," in other words, by either GO or SES incumbents. (See pages 30–31.)

- Using these flexibilities in the GO/SES boundary, career progression can be enhanced in both the GO and SES segments of the senior leader force. (See pages 31–32.)

- A DSS can help to more systematically manage the assignments of GOs. (See pages 44–45.)

Acknowledgments

Our work could not have succeeded without the explicit support of two successive Chiefs of Staff of the Air Force—Gen Michael E. Ryan and Gen John Jumper—and the concurrence of the top echelons of the Air Force's general officers and Senior Executive Service members. Our thinking was shaped significantly through discussions with Gen Billy Boles (USAF, retired) and the late Gen Robert Dixon (USAF, retired). Mr. Roger Blanchard, Assistant Deputy Chief of Staff for Personnel, was instrumental in helping us shape our analysis regarding the Senior Executive Service. Brig Gen Rich Hassan, Director of the Air Force Senior Leader Management Office, provided steadfast direction and support, with able assistance from Lt Cols Cheryl Daly and Cassie Barlow, Majs Brian Kelly and Tony Novello, Capt Gwen Rutherford, Mr. John Service, and Ms. Katrina Jones. Our RAND colleagues who made important contributions to the project included Louis Miller, Richard Stanton, Ray Conley, Wendy Richman Hirsch, Mike Thirtle, Brent Thomas, Jody Paul, Rafal Szczyrba, and Mitch Tuller. Meg Harrell and Mike Hix provided thoughtful reviews.

Acronyms

AFGOMO	Air Force General Officer Matters Office
AFSEMO	Air Force Senior Executive Matters Office
AFSLMO	Air Force Senior Leader Management Office
C2ISR	command, control, intelligence, surveillance, and reconnaissance
CMDB	Command Manpower Database
DSS	decision support system
ERB	Executive Resources Board
FY	fiscal year
GO	general officer
IG	inspector general
KSAO	knowledge, skills, abilities, and other characteristics
LTO	long-term objective
OPM	(U.S.) Office of Personnel Management
PAF	Project AIR FORCE
SAPA	Succession Analysis and Planning Assistant
SES	Senior Executive Service

1. Background

Soon after becoming Chief of Staff of the Air Force in 1998, Gen Michael E. Ryan observed a mismatch between the qualifications of Air Force general officers (GOs) and some of the jobs they needed to fill. He found too few candidates with backgrounds appropriate for filling senior warfighting positions.[1] He also saw many GOs with backgrounds too specialized to be very useful for future positions at higher grades. He asked RAND Project Air Force (PAF), a division of the RAND Corporation, to study the problem and recommend ways of improving the match between future GOs' qualifications and the jobs they must fill.

The structure that was the focus of General Ryan's concern includes approximately 255 line GOs arrayed in four grades: brigadier general (O-7), major general (O-8), lieutenant general (O-9), and general (O-10).[2] Since there are usually more than 255 GO jobs to fill, some jobs must be filled with colonels (O-6s) who have already been selected for promotion to brigadier general. Each officer is assigned to one of approximately 180 Air Force or 80 joint positions (from among a much larger number of joint positions that are filled at different times by flag officers from different military services). GO positions are not aligned with specific Air Force specialties, but many of them have been filled historically by officers with specific career backgrounds (e.g., fighter pilots, civil engineers, acquisition managers).

In addition to relying on the GO force to meet its senior leadership needs, the Air Force relies on approximately 160 career members of the Senior Executive Service (SES).[3] The SES consists of a single pay grade with six pay rates, or steps. Federal agencies are allowed great flexibility in determining pay rates for individual SES members, so SES pay rates do not inherently correlate with the responsibility and authority of an incumbent's job, as is the case with GO grades and jobs. Additionally, there is no natural patterning of career paths, as is afforded by the

---

[1] The goal stated then and adopted in our analyses was that there be at least three qualified candidates eligible for consideration whenever a vacancy had to be filled. In subsequent chapters, we refer to the ratio of jobs to be filled to qualified candidates as *assignment selectivity*.

[2] *Line* is understood in this context to exclude officers in the medical, chaplain, and judge advocate general promotion categories.

[3] This count also includes the relatively small number of members of the Senior Intelligence Executive Service working within the Department of the Air Force. Throughout the text, when we use the term *SES*, we intend that it also include the Senior Intelligence Executive Service.

GO grade structure. Recognizing a need for such patterning, the Air Force has aligned its SES jobs into a four-tier structure based on scope of responsibility and roughly comparable to the GO grade structure.[4] The resulting pyramids define patterns of job progression that enhance development of needed senior leader competencies. Additionally, pay rates and potential bonus levels are linked to job tier. This alignment provides financial incentives for senior executives to accept the organizational and geographical mobility required to progress through the pyramids. Figure 1.1 illustrates how GO grades and SES tiers are aligned in a job progression pyramid.[5]

To illustrate his concern, General Ryan sketched the diagram shown as Figure 1.2 and asked whether the Air Force was creating an appropriate mix of *generalists*, *semi-specialists*, and *specialists* in its GO force. He used the term *generalists* to refer to individuals with experience in the core functions of the Air Force, primarily aircraft operations. Individuals with these backgrounds are generally considered most suitable for filling the most senior GO positions. *Semi-specialists* is the term for line managers with experience in functions such as space, logistics, civil

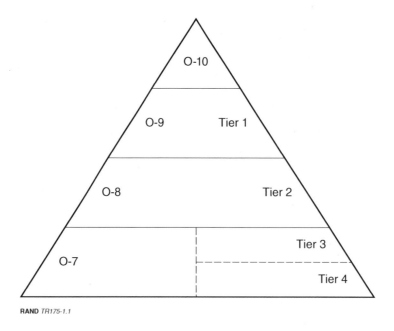

RAND *TR175-1.1*

Figure 1.1—Alignment of GO Grades and SES Tiers

---

[4] To our knowledge, no other federal agency has aligned its SES force in this manner.

[5] The absence of a tier corresponding to grade O-10 does not mean that civilians do not occupy comparable positions. However, all civilian positions at this level are filled by political appointees rather than career members of the SES.

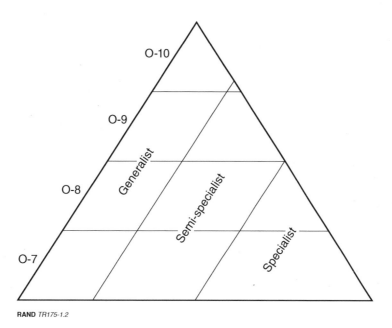

Figure 1.2—An Early Conceptualization: Pyramid of GO Generalists, Semi-specialists, and Specialists

engineering, personnel management, and financial management, which are less central to Air Force missions. Individuals with these backgrounds generally fill positions corresponding to their functional qualifications, which are typically at grades O-9 and below. *Specialists* was what he called individuals in the traditional professions (legal, medical, and chaplain), for which the relevant positions are at grade O-8 and below. He saw the need for more generalists and fewer semi-specialists in the GO corps, and for semi-specialists with greater operational awareness.

In an initial analysis, and working together closely, the Air Force General Officer Matters Office (AFGOMO)[6] and PAF developed a database that delineated numerous areas of knowledge, specific skills, experiences, and innate abilities considered important for each position that an Air Force GO could fill. These included GO positions within the Air Force, of course, as well as joint positions that the Air Force shares with the other services. Statistical analysis[7] of the data sorted the positions into groups that required similar backgrounds. After categorizing each current and anticipated future job as requiring either a

---

[6] In 2001, AFGOMO merged with the Senior Executive Matters Office (AFSEMO), which managed the civilian force of senior executives, whose grades were roughly equivalent to GOs, to become the Air Force Senior Leader Management Office (AFSLMO).

[7] Cluster analysis organized the positions into groups requiring similar combinations of knowledge, skills, and abilities.

generalist, a semi-specialist, or a specialist, we calculated for each category and grade a measure of promotion selectivity: the ratio between (a) the number of GOs eligible for promotion to the grade and (b) the number of promotions into the grade needed per year (to replace those retiring or promoted to the next higher grade). We found notably lower promotion selectivity in the generalist category, both at the time of the analysis and for the future, especially at the higher GO grades.

While that analysis was relatively coarse, we were able to draw several key conclusions from it:

- Selectivity would be increased if GOs had broader backgrounds and thus could serve effectively in a wider range of positions.

- Many GOs needed greater appreciation of Air Force and joint combat and support operations in order to serve effectively in an environment becoming increasingly expeditionary and joint.

- Categorization of GO positions and officers as generalists, semi-specialists, and specialists served a useful interim purpose, but it was inadequate both for expressing goals for the development of future GOs and for analyzing the flows and allocations of officers within the GO force.[8]

Upon reviewing these conclusions in 1999, senior Air Force leadership asked PAF to develop a more detailed framework for describing the backgrounds required in various GO positions. Simultaneously, the leadership created a new staff activity to work toward developing future generations of senior leaders whose backgrounds would allow greater selectivity and would align better with their jobs' competency requirements.[9]

In response, PAF sought to address the following problems and issues:

- To reach a better understanding of the background requirements of GO positions, there would have to be a comprehensive competency framework. Within this framework, the requirements for each position would have to be determined with a reasonable level of fidelity and reliability.

---

[8] Our research revealed that many of the Air Force's most senior and critical positions would be best characterized as requiring not general, nonspecific backgrounds but, rather, multiple specific operational or functional competencies.

[9] The new staff activity was organized during most of 2001 and 2002 as the Developing Aerospace Leaders Program Office. It was later incorporated as a division within AFSLMO and then, more recently, transferred to the Directorate of Strategic Plans and Future Systems (AF/DPX).

- In a closed personnel system, all positions are filled by the cohorts of individuals who pass through entry-level selection processes. For GO positions, these cohorts consist of the relatively small number of colonels selected each year for promotion to brigadier general. To minimize learning on the job, these cohorts should come as close as possible to supplying all the competencies needed in all GO positions. Accordingly, an optimal and feasible distribution of competencies in these cohorts is needed as a template for developing pools of highly qualified candidates.

- A significant part of the Air Force's need for senior leadership is met by members of the Senior Executive Service (SES). Career members of the SES occupy jobs that are comparable to those filled by military officers in grades from colonel to lieutenant general.[10] While these SES members do not formally command military units, they may serve as directors or deputy directors of non-warfighting organizations and staff elements, as well as in a variety of specialized staff positions. Many have prepared for their positions through lengthy careers within the Department of the Air Force. To fully address Air Force senior leader needs, leader development and selectivity had to be looked at not only within the GO force, but within the Air Force's senior civil service workforce as well.

- In the past, GO and SES positions were considered relatively fixed. However, some flexibility in the choice of whether to use GO or SES members to fill specific positions might enhance the management of both the GO and the SES workforces.

- The Air Force is limited in the number of GOs and SES members it may have on its rolls. It must allocate these scarce resources to specific organizations and activities so as to meet the current leadership needs while also providing opportunities to further develop individuals for the highest GO and SES levels. An understanding of GO and SES career progression needs could inform this resource allocation process.

- Determining GO and SES competency requirements for the purpose of developing future leaders with those competencies yields a rich database that, if married to information on the competencies of current GOs and SES members, could be used to help manage the ongoing utilization and further development of these resources.

This report describes the analytic steps taken by PAF to address these issues. Chapter Two describes how the database of competencies required for the GO

---

[10] For protocol purposes, all SES members are considered equivalent to general officers—i.e., they are all considered to be at Distinguished Visitor Code 6 or higher.

and SES jobs was developed and analyzed. Chapter Three describes a new modeling framework that uses occupational/functional competency information from this database, reflects personnel flows and allocations, and derives optimal mixes of competencies in the annual cohorts of colonels selected for promotion to brigadier general and civilians selected for entry into the SES. Chapter Four examines the boundary between GO and SES use and describes analyses leading to some useful flexibilities in employing GOs and SES members to fill certain positions. Chapter Five describes an analysis of how these flexibilities can be used to enhance the development and use of both GO and SES senior leader resources. Chapter Six introduces concepts for a decision support system (DSS) that could enhance the management of senior leaders. Chapter Seven summarizes our work's implications for the Air Force and the other services.

2. Understanding the Competency Requirements of USAF Senior Leader Jobs

Although specific backgrounds are not critical for all GO and SES positions, they are critical for many. For example, it is critical that a Joint Forces Air Component Commander (JFACC) have a fighter or bomber background and be thoroughly steeped in the employment of air and space power.[1] And it is critical that an incumbent assigned as the Assistant Deputy Chief of Staff for Personnel on the Air Staff (an SES position) have a background in Air Force manpower and personnel management. Although the requirements for such positions may be known by, among others, the Secretary of the Air Force and the Chief of Staff, such knowledge alone does not ensure that there will be enough appropriately skilled senior leaders to choose from when one of these positions needs to be filled. Identifying the skills each senior leader position requires makes it possible to plan the development and assignment of senior leaders so as to minimize the occurrence of the selectivity problems described in Chapter One. Prior to the research being discussed here, this information was not available to the Air Force. In a sense, because the specific skill requirements for senior leader positions had never been well defined, the Air Force had no way to systematically develop an inventory of senior leaders to fill such positions.

This chapter describes the steps taken to develop and analyze a database of the skills required for USAF and Joint GO and SES positions.

Defining Position Requirements

Job analysts distinguish between the tasks that a job incumbent performs and the knowledge, skills, abilities, and other characteristics (KSAO) he/she needs to perform those tasks successfully. Tasks are observable, whereas KSAO are derived by inference. For example, one may more readily observe that a position requires the creation of a five-year plan (an observable task) than that a position requires someone who is "visionary" (a nonobservable characteristic). Analysts

---

[1] The Department of Defense (DoD) has organized joint regional commands for the purpose of employing combat forces. Within each regional command, the JFACC exercises operational control of theater air assets allocated to the command.

would prefer to focus on observable behaviors to ensure, as much as possible, that the results of a job analysis are reliable and valid. If behaviors cannot be directly observed, however, an analyst has two choices: describe jobs in terms of the tasks to be performed and then draw inferences about the KSAO required to perform those tasks, or describe jobs directly in terms of the KSAO required. In either case, someone must draw inferences about the KSAO required for the job. Since directly observing the large number of unique senior leader jobs in the Air Force would have been prohibitively expensive, we chose the second approach for this analysis, relying primarily on incumbents and former incumbents to report the KSAO required for their positions.

A complicating factor in our analysis is that job requirements are not immutable. Ilgen and Hollenbeck (1991) observed that "jobs exist in an environment that is *subjective, personal, and dynamic.*" Although a cluster of tasks may be formally designated for a position, the inherently individual nature of jobs lets task elements result in part from personalization of the job. Morrison and Hock (1986) observed that this phenomenon is especially prevalent in more-senior positions. That is, while positions may have core elements that remain essentially unchanged over long periods, they also have personalized elements that change not only from incumbent to incumbent, but from time to time for each incumbent. This suggests that any snapshot of a position's KSAO requirements will show relatively slower-changing core elements, potentially rapidly changing requirements unique to a given point in time, and requirements related to the incumbent's unique personalization of the job. All of these elements are reflected in the results of a job analysis, including the one reported here. As discussed below, the distinction between core and noncore elements may explain some differences among raters in the results we obtained.

Developing a Job Analysis Questionnaire

As the first step in creating a database of the qualifications required for senior leader positions, we—together with Air Force GOs and the leadership of AFGOMO—constructed a list of KSAO potentially required for GO positions (see Appendix A). This list was refined iteratively with a sample of GOs to ensure that it was comprehensive enough to describe all USAF GO position requirements. The KSAO considered critical for all GO positions (e.g., personal integrity and various leadership skills) were not included in the list, our assumption being that any individual rising to the rank of GO will, by virtue of having been chosen for that rank, already possess them.

We organized the final list of KSAO into a questionnaire that AFGOMO sent during 1999 to all GOs then serving in line USAF GO positions.[2] For each position, we tried to obtain a completed questionnaire from the current and previous incumbents. Respondents first rated each of 109 specific KSAO (listed in Table A.1 in Appendix A) as "critical," "important," "useful," or "not applicable" to performance in their position. Next, they judged whether the KSAO requirement also could be met by someone in a "partnered" position. For example, if a skill was judged "critical" to performance but the requirement could be met by a deputy with that skill, then it was marked as a "partnered" skill. Finally, respondents judged whether each of the KSAO would become more or less important for the position five years hence. Because the Chief of Staff emphasized the need to respond to the questionnaire, we achieved a 100 percent response rate and received more than one response (i.e., incumbent and previous incumbent) for 95 positions.

Later, in 2000, we developed a similar questionnaire for SES positions and administered it to incumbents in all positions except those known to be temporary and those occupied by political appointees.[3] Although we made some changes in the SES version to accommodate differences between the GO and SES environments,[4] we maintained essential uniformity between the GO and SES versions in order to facilitate a comparison of the two segments of the senior leadership structure.

Initial Survey Response Analyses

We took the following steps to prepare survey response data for analysis:

---

[2] Initially, questionnaires were not sent to USAF GOs assigned to joint positions because the Air Force was reluctant to task them for responses. For these positions, competencies needed for immediate analysis were initially determined by the GOMO staff and later refined through an abbreviated version of the questionnaire sent to the incumbents. Positions in the medical, chaplain, and judge advocate general corps were excluded because these positions are not filled from the larger pool of line officers, which means that the requirements for these positions are not relevant to the development of line officers.

[3] The information obtained in the questionnaire was intended for use in developing future senior leaders. Accordingly, we sought information only for positions likely to be filled later by individuals currently serving at lower grades in the Air Force civil service workforce. Political appointees generally are not drawn from this pool.

[4] For example, we modified the list of functional area backgrounds that might be critical, important, or useful to include those where SES members typically have experience, and to exclude those that can only be gained through military experience.

- For GO positions, we reviewed raters' responses and compared and synthesized[5] them with prior PAF and AFGOMO judgments.[6]

- For SES positions, panels of senior SES members with the suitable functional backgrounds reviewed raters' responses.

- For GO positions, a lieutenant general or equivalent in the position's chain of command reviewed the synthesized data.

- We further synthesized results from these reviews.

- AFGOMO and AFSEMO reviewed and finalized the data for analysis.

Analyses to develop a conceptual framework for describing senior leader position requirements included basic tabulations, cluster analysis of positions, and factor analysis of the survey items.

Each step is described in detail below.

Reliability

Because we used an iterative process to assign the final ratings to all of the KSAO for each position, we could not directly examine the reliability of the final ratings. However, we had two sets of ratings for 95 positions among the original GO questionnaires, and we were able to examine the extent of agreement among these 95 pairs of raters' original responses. For these analyses, we calculated agreement indices only for KSAO that at least one rater had reported as required for the job. This eliminated spuriously high correlations that would arise from perfect agreement about KSAO not required for the job (Harvey, 1991).[7]

The average correlation between raters across the entire survey for these 95 positions was $r = .36$, indicating questionable agreement among raters. The maximum correlation between raters was $r = .63$, and the minimum correlation between raters was $r = 0$. This outcome is not particularly surprising, since the raters' familiarities with a position represented two distinct points in time. As we noted above, it is not uncommon for elements of a job to change over time.

---

[5] Synthesis consisted of comparing the multiple responses received from the GO incumbents and their predecessors, and making a judgment as to what to record for the position. The emphasis was primarily on identifying and correcting outlying responses.

[6] At a very early stage of the project, PAF and AFGOMO representatives rated each GO position against a prior list of KSAO developed for this purpose.

[7] One might reasonably argue that two raters choosing to say that a skill is not required for a position should be reflected as agreement. Our decision to exclude this kind of agreement from the calculation of inter-rater reliability is conservative. It gives a lower-bound estimate of agreement.

However, this mutability does highlight the need for maintaining up-to-date KSAO requirements for each job.

Correlations were higher for the first three sections of the questionnaire, which addressed the position's requirements for experience in various functional management domains (e.g., acquisition, personnel) and broad categories of Air Force operations (e.g., fighter, bomber, airlift). The average correlation between raters for these sections was $r = .48$, with a maximum of $r = .79$ and a minimum of $r = -.19$. We hypothesize that these correlations are higher than those discussed above because a position's operational and functional requirements are core elements and thus likely to change slowly over time, if at all. Consequently, it is not surprising that the reliability for judgments on the criticality of these requirements is higher. The inter-rater agreement on requirements for the third section of the questionnaire alone (addressing operational knowledge and operational credibility) was even higher, with an average inter-rater agreement of $r = .63$.

We further hypothesize that the requirements for which agreement was substantially lacking represent either fleeting but potentially recurring requirements of the positions or personalized aspects of the positions that depend on the specific incumbents who responded to the questionnaires. In any case, the functional and operational requirements for these positions, which are the basis for most of the analysis reported in this document, were more reliably measured than were the other requirements in the questionnaire.

Developing a Conceptual Framework

In reviewing the initial survey responses, we began to concentrate on operational and functional requirements. As indicated above, the data on these requirements exhibited far better reliability than did other data obtained in the GO survey. Further, we reasoned that depth in operational and functional competencies is gained primarily through experience in or with the operational or functional area, whereas other KSAO are either innate or can be gained through various combinations of experience, training, education, and mentoring. Far greater long-term planning and far more opportunity costs are associated with the deliberate development of competencies through the management of experience (i.e., through the management of job rotations and career patterns) rather than through other means. We believed that the most important initial contribution our research could make toward better development of senior leaders for the Air Force was to articulate the requirements for operational and functional experience and construct a template for how they might be met.

The initial GO survey data identified the need for knowledge of an average of five critical operational or functional areas per position. We reasoned that most officers could not be expected to gain direct experience working in five different operational or functional areas during the approximately twenty years available to develop them for senior leader jobs. We felt that there would be exceptions, but that most officers (especially rated officers) could obtain noteworthy experience in no more than two operational or functional areas. We thus recommended that operational and functional background requirements be differentiated as follows.

First, *primary* and *secondary occupational competency requirements* are those requirements that demand an operational or functional background at the depth that can be gained only through direct, occupational experience within the operational or functional area, as a *provider* of the product or service of the function. The *primary* occupational competency is the one considered the most critical to success in the job; the *secondary* occupational competency, if specified, is less critical. Second, critical knowledge of other operational or functional areas need not be at an occupational or service-provider level. The *familiarity* that is gained, either as a consumer of the products or services of the operational or functional area or through education or training, suffices.

Deriving Primary and Secondary Skill Requirements

Using the questionnaire responses, the officer in charge of AFSLMO (in consultation with AFSLMO staff and RAND analysts) and the panels that reviewed SES positions identified the one or two most critical occupational or functional backgrounds that would be considered the primary and secondary occupational competency requirements for each position. As PAF and AFSLMO gained experience with this format, the list of primary and secondary occupational competencies evolved, and it may continue to evolve as the data become more commonly used. A recent version of the list is in Table 2.1. The Occupational Competencies column shows both *basic competencies*, which are for a single functional or operational area (e.g., "fighter" or "acquisition management") and *bins*, which are for broader or more flexible competencies (e.g., "any rated" or "fighter, bomber, or mobility").[8] Each row in the table identifies either a single basic competency (shown in roman type) or a single bin competency (shown in italics).

---

[8] We developed the concept of *bins* to recognize that for some positions, several different skill sets are equally acceptable. For example, the "fighter or bomber" bin admits that either a fighter or a bomber pilot can fill some positions, and the "any" bin admits that some positions are completely flexible with respect to occupational background.

Table 2.1

Primary and Secondary Occupational Competencies

Occupational Competency[a]	GO	SES
Any	X	X
Any rated	X	X
Fighter	X	
Bomber	X	
Mobility	X	
C2ISR (rated)	X	
Experimental/test	X	X
Special operations	X	
Fighter, bomber, or mobility	X	X
Fighter or bomber	X	X
Fighter, bomber, or C2ISR	X	X
Fighter, bomber, mobility, or space	X	X
Missile or bomber	X	X
Air power employment	X	X
Mobility operations	X	X
Bomber, missile, or space	X	X
Acquisition management	X	X
Test and evaluation	X	X
Contracting	X	X
Laboratory science and engineering		X
Product support engineering	X	X
Any acquisition	X	X
Any acquisition or logistics	X	X
Any acquisition or maintenance	X	X
Any science & engineering or program management	X	X
Any science or engineering	X	X
Maintenance	X	X
Logistics	X	X
Any financial management		X
Accounting and finance	X	X
Budget		X
Cost and management analysis		X
Audit		X
Any financial management or logistics	X	X
Any financial management or civil engineering	X	X
Accounting and finance or any acquisition or logistics	X	X
Manpower and personnel	X	X
Education/training	X	X
Space employment	X	X
Missile	X	
Space employment or missile	X	X
Information operations	X	X
C2ISR (nonrated)	X	X
Communications/computers	X	X
Civil engineering	X	X
Services		X

14

Table 2.1—continued

Occupational Competency[a]	GO	SES
Administration		X
History		X
Operations research		X
Force protection	X	
Inspector general (IG)[b]		
IG or force protection	X	X
Office of Special Investigations (OSI)	X	X
Intelligence	X	X
Intelligence or contracting	X	X
Intelligence or military personnel/manpower or civilian personnel/manpower	X	X
Safety		X
Nuclear weapons	X	X
Plans and programs	X	X
Political-military affairs	X	
International relations/security assistance	X	X
Weather	X	X
Air operations support		X
Legal		X
Requirements	X	X
Public affairs	X	
War planning (e.g., J-5, A-5)	X	

NOTE: An X in the GO or SES column indicates that the competency is applicable to that category.

[a] Basic competencies are shown in roman type; bins are in italics. (See text for definitions.)

[b] "*IG*" is a valid functional competency, but in the set of jobs used to compile this list it does not appear as a basic requirement for any GO or SES job. However, it does appear as part of a bin requirement, "*IG or force protection*" (see the next row in the table).

Functional Familiarities

As noted, functional familiarities represent knowledge of operational or functional areas at a sub-occupational level, the level needed for the incumbent to be a well-informed consumer of the operational or functional areas' products or services. These were drawn directly from the questionnaire and potentially include any of the occupational competencies listed in Table 2.1.

Cross-Functional Competencies

In addition to functional and operational skills, the questionnaire included items related to topics such as budgeting, geographical knowledge, and communication and management skills. Because these items represent KSAO that cut across traditional functional areas rather than being uniquely developed by individuals in specific Air Force functional specialties (as, for example, a skill such as piloting a fighter aircraft), we call them "cross-functional" competencies. We factor-analyzed these items from the GO survey (Nunnally, 1978) and retained the eleven factors shown in Table 2.2.[9] We analyzed the SES surveys similarly, and although the results were not identical, we judged them similar enough to warrant using the same cross-functional competencies for both GOs and SESs.

Table 2.2

Cross-Competency Factors

Factor Number	Factor
I	Management
II	Operational awareness
III	Analytic skill
IV	Geopolitical awareness
V	Resource management
VI	Communication skill
VII	Policy and planning
VIII	Command and headquarters experience
IX	Civilian management
X	Non-DoD agency awareness
XI	Space operational awareness

Refresher Surveys

During 2003, we and AFSLMO developed refresher surveys and administered them to incumbents of GO and SES positions. These surveys differed in both content and form from the questionnaires used in the initial GO and SES position surveys. This time we asked respondents to specifically identify primary occupational, secondary occupational, and familiarity requirements for operational/functional backgrounds and to use our previously identified factors rather than more-detailed items to reflect cross-functional competency requirements. AFSLMO administered the surveys electronically, using a Web-based instrument for the GO survey and a spreadsheet-based instrument, sent and returned as an e-mail attachment, for the SES survey. Plans were made to

---

[9] We used an iterated principal-factor approach and then a varimax rotation. A scree plot informed our choice of how many factors to retain. The eleven-factor solution made the most sense conceptually. Appendix A lists the individual items and the factors where they "load."

administer a refresher survey at a measured interval after a new incumbent has been assigned to a position so that the database would be continuously updated.

Positions Considered

In deciding which positions to consider, we excluded those that would not be fed by the broad, general development programs that were the focus of the analysis. The following positions were excluded:

- GO medical, chaplain, and judge advocate general positions
- Political appointee positions in the SES grades
- Temporary positions
- Positions not in the *objective force*.[10]

The counts of positions used in the analysis include joint billets (positions in the Office of the Secretary of Defense [OSD], the Joint Staff, the Joint commands, and the Defense agencies), but at the Air Force's expected fill rate. If a joint job is filled continuously by the Air Force, we counted it as a full position. If a job is rotated among the Air Force and one or more other services, we counted it as half, a third, or a fourth of a position, as appropriate. In these position counts, expected values rather than simple counts are analytically sound.

The need for secondary occupational competencies is quite high. In a recently examined set of Air Force jobs, 88 percent of the GO positions and 66 percent of the SES positions were found to require a secondary competency.

Each position requires a unique array of functional familiarities and cross-functional competencies. Although these data are not exploited in the flow analyses reported in this document, they provide insights for the Air Force to use in planning for the development of future GOs. Future work may focus greater analytic attention on these requirements.

---

[10] AFSLMO generally sees more position requirements than inventory. The subset of required positions designated to be filled with available inventory is referred to as the *objective force*.

3. Modeling Career Progression

As discussed earlier, in Chapter One, an understanding of the competency requirements of individual positions is, by itself, insufficient for determining development needs. Moreover, in a closed personnel system, it may be impossible to develop an inventory of senior leaders that meets all competency requirements, particularly when the requirements are for operational or functional experience that can be fully developed only through job rotations. In this chapter, we describe an analytic approach that allows the operational and functional requirements of individual senior leader jobs to be translated into an optimal and feasible distribution of such competencies in entering cohorts of brigadier general and SES selectees. These optimal distributions become templates for developing pools of highly competitive officers and civilians from which to choose future GO and SES entry cohorts.

Chapter Two indicates that many positions require individuals who possess depth in more than one operational or functional competency. These positions can be said to require *simultaneous* multifunctionality. Further, the *pyramids* associated with many competencies are not readily structured to promote reasonable career progression through the GO grades or SES tiers. If the positions are grouped by primary occupational competency, many groups, arrayed by grade or tier, will form broad-based pyramids (i.e., a relatively large number of lower-grade or lower-tier positions for each higher-grade or higher-tier position). Other groups will form narrow-based pyramids (i.e., relatively few lower-grade or lower-tier positions for each higher-grade or higher-tier position). Figure 3.1 depicts, for the GO case, several alternative shapes that might be observed in these occupational competency pyramids. If it is assumed that the Air Force would like to maintain reasonably consistent promotion opportunity across these pyramids, individuals with primary competencies in narrow-based pyramids must be qualified for and "banked" in the lower grades of broad-based pyramids.[1] This provides larger pools of officers to compete for O-9 and O-10 positions, thus enhancing selectivity. The shape of the pyramids can become

---

[1] We use the term *banking* to indicate the use of an individual in a position that does not specifically call for his/her primary occupational competency. One form of banking is to place an individual in one of the broader bins listed in Table 2.1. Another form is to use an individual's secondary occupational competency as a match for the primary occupational competency requirement of a position (which is identified as "match quality 2"—see Table 3.3, below).

18

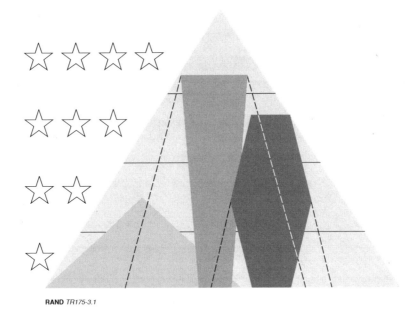

RAND *TR175-3.1*

**Figure 3.1—Alternative Shapes of Occupational Competency Pyramids
Within the Overall GO Pyramid**

more distorted when primary/secondary pairings of occupational competencies
are considered. When there are jobs that require individuals to have different
competencies as they progress through grades or tiers, the system can be said to
require *serial* multifunctionality.

The objective of the methodology we describe here was to determine the ideal
patterns of multifunctionality among cohorts of O-6s promoted to O-7 and
civilians promoted into the SES, along with appropriate utilization and
promotion of such cohorts as they reach higher grades and tiers. Ideal patterns
would provide the best possible fit of *faces* to *spaces*—i.e., the best possible
matching of individual competencies to job requirements—across all grades and
tiers. The methodology can help the decisionmaker trade off competing
competency and assignment selectivity demands. One ultimate purpose is to
provide a target for developing appropriate multifunctionality among the
officers and civilians who will eventually compete for promotion to the GO and
SES ranks—in other words, among the highly competitive officers and civilians.

We used a linear-programming model representing an ideal steady state to
derive optimal competency mixes. We refer to it as a *flow model* because it reflects
the flows of individuals through the various GO grades or SES tiers. Each
position is characterized by its GO grade (O-7 through O-10) or SES tier (4

through 1), the primary occupational competency required, and, if applicable, the secondary occupational competency required.[2] Positions may be referred to as *spaces* in the model. The model also generates notional *faces*—a virtual inventory of individuals, described by primary/secondary competency mixes within each grade, that can best fill the *spaces*.

Actual inventories of GOs and SES members are not used in the model. Rather, the model solves for an ideal inventory that can be used as a benchmark against which actual inventories may be compared, and as a template for guiding the development of individuals competitive for future GO and SES selections.

Mathematical Underpinnings

The model has two fundamental mathematical underpinnings. First, in one aspect it assumes the general form of a *transportation* model, whose classical purpose was to determine the least-cost combination of moves of goods from a number of sources to a number of destinations, given maximum production capacities at the various sources, consumption requirements at the various destinations, and a matrix of transportation costs for each possible source-to-destination movement. In our flow model, the personnel inventory categories (faces) are equivalent to sources, the categories of jobs (spaces) are equivalent to destinations, and the quality match score fillmap (see below) corresponds to the cost matrix.

The second mathematical underpinning is Little's Theorem,[3] which in our application states that the number of individuals (n) in a grade/tier must equal the product of the annual promotions (p) into the grade/tier and the average time in the grade/tier (t), or:

$$n = p * t.$$

This relationship holds for the aggregate grade/tier and for the primary/secondary occupational competency pairings within the grade/tier. For each primary/secondary pair, the model knows the number of positions associated with that pair and the average time anyone with that pair will spend in the grade/tier. It can then readily determine the number of promotions needed to keep the positions filled.

---

[2] The flow model does not represent each position or person individually. Instead, it represents the sum of requirements or people with each combination of grade/tier, primary competency, and secondary competency.

[3] John D.C. Little (1961) provided the first rigorous proof of this theorem.

The mathematical work is to simultaneously ascertain (1) how much of each primary/secondary requirement at each grade/tier should be filled using each primary/secondary category of person, and (2) how many people with each primary/secondary pair should be promoted from each grade/tier to the next.

Matching Faces and Spaces: The *Fillmap*

Ideally, the Air Force wants an individual who fills a position to have the primary and secondary occupational competencies that the position needs. In reality, however, the imperfect career progression pyramids (see description, above) sometimes rule out the ideal. If we consider the feasible and desirable flows of individuals through the GO grades and SES tiers and assume that it is generally infeasible for most individuals to gain reasonable depth in more than two functional areas, there is no way to obtain a perfect match of faces to spaces. However, if we employ a scoring system to differentiate the relative quality of various faces-to-spaces matches, optimization can find ideal inventories with optimal fit—the best overall sum of match qualities across all requirements.

Table 3.1 indicates the basic match quality scoring scheme used in the model. In this scheme, a match quality of 1 indicates a perfect match: the primary and secondary competencies on the faces side match, respectively, the primary and secondary competencies on the spaces side. Less desirable match patterns have increasingly higher match quality scores, up to a score of 5. Matches inferior to the least-desirable (5) entry are not identified in the fillmap and are not allowed in model solutions. The model's objective function is the weighted sum of such match qualities over all requirements. The model attempts to *minimize* this sum.

Table 3.1

Illustrative Match Quality Scores

Occupational Competency of Virtual Inventory		Match Quality Score
Primary	Secondary	
Matches required primary	Matches required secondary	1
Matches required secondary	Matches required primary	2
Matches required primary	Related to, but not a perfect match for, required secondary	3
Matches required primary	Unrelated to required secondary	4
Unrelated to required primary or secondary	Matches required primary	5

While results are generally reported using this basic scheme, the model is often run with match quality scores that are weighted differently. In some cases, higher weights are assigned to higher grades or tiers. In other cases, higher weights are assigned to poorer match qualities. In any of these cases, higher weights increase the penalties for poorer matches. While we found no empirical basis for assigning weights, higher weights for higher grades/tiers seem intuitively appropriate, because positions in higher grades/tiers have a greater impact on organizational performance. They produced results that Air Force senior leader managers viewed as superior to results obtained with even weights across the grades/tiers.

Table 3.2 provides notional examples of match quality scores for a variety of requirements when the virtual inventory's primary occupational competency is *fighter* and the secondary is *acquisition management*. The full matrix of such scores for all required primary/secondary competency pairs and all applicable combinations of inventory competencies is referred to as a *fillmap*. The model uses the fillmap matrix, developed in a preparatory step before running the model, to assign match quality scores to potential faces-to-spaces alignments.

Table 3.2

Typical Match Quality Scores:
Inventory Primary Occupational Competency = Fighter;
Inventory Secondary Occupational Competency = Acquisition Management

Required Occupational Competency		Match Quality Score
Primary	Secondary	
Rated	None	1
Rated	Acquisition management	1
Fighter	None	1
Fighter	Acquisition management	1
Fighter or bomber	None	1
Fighter or bomber	Acquisition management	1
Fighter, bomber, or mobility	None	1
Fighter, bomber, or mobility	Acquisition management	1
Acquisition management	None	2
Acquisition management	Fighter	2
Any rated	Contracting	3
Fighter	Air power employment	4
Acquisition management	Mobility	5

Model Constraints

The model incorporates a series of constraints that govern the flow of virtual faces through spaces, as represented in a model solution, to represent with some degree of authenticity the actual flow of real faces through spaces at various grades/tiers. The important constraints are described in the following paragraphs.

Promotion Constraints

Because the model represents a steady state, the number of promotions *into* a grade must exactly equal the total flows (retirements and promotions) out of the grade. Parameters representing overall targets for these rates of promotion flows must be entered into the flow model. For both the GO and the SES module of the flow model, these parameters are derived from other, aggregate-level models of behavior within the GO and SES promotion/advancement systems.

The GO and SES promotion/advancement systems differ in some important respects. GO assignments and promotions are closely and centrally managed through formal promotion boards (for promotion to brigadier general and major general), senate confirmations, and the close personal attention of Air Force senior leadership. As a result, promotion and career progression parameters are well understood and, in many respects, carefully controlled through central management mechanisms. In contrast, SES assignment and promotion decisions are largely left to the purview of supervisors of the affected positions. While SES appointments are subject to oversight by the Air Force's Executive Resources Board (ERB) and the U.S. Office of Personnel Management (OPM), the SES system does not strictly demand the degree of central management and control found in the GO system.[4] Additionally, because the Air Force created the tier system, it can and does exercise flexibility in using lateral entries from outside the Air Force, advancements that skip tiers, and initial SES appointments to positions above tier 4—career progression patterns that are impermissible in the more rigid, GO grade structure.

The Air Force GO force is structured so that about two-thirds of the O-7 selectees are ultimately selected for promotion to O-8, about half of the O-8 selectees are ultimately promoted to O-9, and about one out of four O-9 promotees are

---

[4] In accordance with 5 USC 3393, an ERB is a body of SES members established within a federal agency to review qualifications of candidates for appointment in the SES and to provide recommendations to the appropriate appointing authority. The ERBs in some agencies, including the Air Force, have also assumed broader roles in managing the SES corps within their agencies.

ultimately promoted to O-10. The flow model constrains the aggregate force to fit these promotion probabilities. The flow model further holds tenure in each grade at observed averages. Specific parameters for promotion probability and average time in grade are derived from the Air Force's aggregate steady-state long-term objective (LTO) inventory projection model.[5]

In the SES version of the flow model, advancement to a higher tier is represented in the same way as a promotion to a higher GO grade. Strictly speaking, there is only one SES grade, so movement between tiers is not a *promotion*. However, the Air Force manages these advancements so that they generally result in a higher level of responsibility and an associated opportunity for a higher level of compensation. Thus, for modeling purposes, these advancements are treated as equivalent to a promotion. The SES version differs from the GO version in that the SES system is not perfectly "closed." In order to advance to the grade of O-8, an officer must first hold the grade of O-7. In contrast, an individual can be promoted into the SES at any tier, either from lower civil service grades or from outside the civil service. Further, individuals within the SES can skip tiers when being reassigned. The model makes allowances for these departures from a closed personnel system, but holds them to a minimum, consistent with actual experience.

Because the central management of GO progressions is intense, our efforts to build a disaggregate (occupational-level) GO flow model were founded on a rich source of historical data and a time-tested aggregate planning model (the LTO model) that helped us understand parameters such as times in grade, selection rates, and promotion probabilities.

For the SES system, we had no similar source of aggregate parameters. The tier system was implemented too recently to provide useful historical data. We could have retroactively matched jobs to tiers in a longitudinal historical file spanning enough years to generate tier progression parameters. However, the tier structure was established to *change* rather than preserve historical job progression patterns, so parameters generated from historical data would be unsuitable for use in formulating SES force management objectives.

In lieu of historical data as a basis for the needed parameters, we constructed an aggregate, steady-state tier progression model, calibrated to the average tenures

---

[5] Inputs to the LTO model include the numbers of officers in each grade, historically based retirement rates at each year in grade, historically based year-of-service promotion distributions, mandatory retirement points, and promotion eligibility policies. Model outputs include numbers of promotions into each grade, average times in each grade (and average times to promotion out of and retirement from each grade), promotion selectivities, and promotion probabilities.

in each tier and selection rates for advancement from tier to tier anticipated by the Air Force's ERB when it established the tier structure. Certain parameters required for this model (initial appointments above tier 4, lateral entries, and advancements that skip tiers) were estimated by examining tier pyramids within primary occupational competencies, refined using the disaggregate SES model, and entered as inputs to the aggregate model. Other parameters (average years in tier and selection rates) were developed using the aggregate model and entered as inputs to the disaggregate SES flow model. We adjusted the two models iteratively until we obtained compatible parameters.

Both models reflect reasonable *promotion* selectivities. These are applied at the primary/secondary occupational competency level and act to ensure, insofar as possible, that there are at least three available candidates with the requisite skill mixes for each promotion/advancement.

Assignment Constraints

The model contains constraints to ensure that all position requirements are filled. Further, the GO version of the model applies a *job selectivity* constraint to ensure that at least three qualified candidates will be available for any job vacancy.

The GO version includes several *shaping* constraints, or intermediate objective functions, whose purpose is to narrow the range of optimal solutions to exclude solutions whose inventories would depart too radically from conventional expectations. One of these affects the distribution of primary competencies in the annual cohort of promotions to grade O-7. Another affects the distribution of secondary competencies within selected primary competencies. The GO version of the model has much more inventory flexibility than the SES version does, primarily because competency requirements tend to be more flexible in GO jobs than in SES jobs (i.e., a large proportion of GO jobs have competency requirements represented by a bin, such as *any rated*). The model could find an optimal solution in which most of these flexible requirements were satisfied using an inventory distribution unlikely to be found in the real world and possibly not robust across changing requirements. The shaping constraints tend to exclude these unusual distributions.

The Solution Space

Given the large numbers of requirements identified by bins, the range of acceptable matches represented in the fillmap, and the flexibility permitted in promotion probabilities, multiple solutions provide equal match quality.

Mathematically, none of these solutions is better than any other. By examining them, we can identify ranges of optimal inventory and promotion values for each primary/secondary competency pair. The model can be configured, for example, to determine the maximum and minimum number in each primary/secondary pairing in the annual O-7 promotion cohort. Methodologically, the objective function (minimizing overall match quality) is converted to a constraint (i.e., overall match quality can be no worse than the optimal level). For each primary/secondary pairing in the entry cohort, a run may seek either the maximum or minimum value for annual O-7 promotions in a specific primary/secondary pairing. Using these runs, the most interesting findings indicate which primary/secondary pairs cannot be reduced to zero. These represent relatively firm requirements. While there is flexibility in other requirements, these nonzero minimum requirements seem irreducibly linked to future organizational performance and selectivity.

While model solutions contain promotion and inventory values and utilization patterns (the assignment of virtual inventory to jobs, or, equivalently, the allocation of jobs to virtual inventory) for all four grades or tiers, the output of greatest interest to many decisionmakers is the distribution of primary/secondary pairings in the cohorts of annual promotions to grade O-7 and into the SES. As mentioned earlier, these distributions provide benchmarks for evaluating the availability of required competencies among either recently selected cohorts or pools of current or future contenders. Further, these ideal distributions can be used to guide the developmental assignments of future contenders.

How Recent Cohorts Compare

We analyzed recent brigadier general promotion board results to see how closely the selectees matched the need for the primary and secondary occupational competency pairs revealed through our analysis. We compared counts of primary and secondary occupational competencies among selectees in five cohorts (those selected in 1996 through 2000) against both the point solutions and the minimums of the entry cohort requirements.[6] We found that most of the minimum requirements for primary occupational competencies were met. However, only about 40 percent of the selectees in these cohorts had secondary

---

[6] The point solution values are the initial results from the linear programming model. The minimum requirements, which are determined through sensitivity analysis, are the lowest levels to which entries in a given primary/secondary pairing can be reduced without reducing overall match quality. To sustain match quality, entries at the minimum level in some pairings must be offset by entries above the point solution in one or more other pairings.

competencies; optimum would be for virtually all of them to have useful secondary competencies.

Development Targets

As a practical matter, AFSLMO and other Air Force activities responsible for developing competitive individuals for future GO and SES promotions do not use the detailed information reflected in the model outputs. They generalize to identify the pairings of primary and secondary occupational competencies that are most prominently required in entering cohorts. Examples are shown in Table 3.3. Tables such as this one send signals about targets for development—for example, that broadening the competencies of *fighter* pilots or weapon system operators into functions such as *airpower employment, political-military*, or *acquisition management* will be useful to the Air Force in meeting future executive needs, whereas broadening them into functions such as *maintenance, logistics*, or *manpower and personnel* will not serve a specific need.

Table 3.3

Typical Primary/Secondary Occupational Pairings as Development Targets

Occupational Competency	GO Example	SES Example
Primary competency	Fighter	Logistics
Useful secondary competencies	Airpower employment	Acquisition management
	Acquisition management	Contracting
	Space	Maintenance
	Political-military	
	Plans and programs	

4. The GO/SES Boundary

One of the issues placed before us was whether flexible use of GO and SES members to fill specific positions could be advantageous for the Air Force. This chapter describes our exploration of this issue.

We first describe similarities and differences in how GOs and SES members are utilized in the Air Force, after which we describe an approach we developed to help the Air Force relax the formerly rather strict boundary between the realms in which GO use and SES use were thought to be appropriate.[1] Finally, we outline in general terms how taking advantage of treating this boundary more flexibly can enhance the career progression of both GO and SES resources.

Differences Between GO and SES Utilization

Important differences between the contexts in which GO and SES resources are typically utilized relate to factors such as military necessity, desired depth and breadth of occupational competencies, and senior leader grade thresholds. We examine each of these differences below.

Military Necessity

Many senior leader jobs in the Air Force are closely bound to core warfighting functions. Law, custom, and practicality generally dictate that these jobs be filled by military incumbents. Jobs requiring the exercise of command over military units are in this category, as are jobs requiring the incumbent to exercise or be subject to the Uniform Code of Military Justice. As a practical matter, some jobs require a competency (e.g., *fighter*) that can be developed only by military members.[2]

---

[1] In exercising these flexibilities, designating billets as military or civilian must be based on manpower mix criteria provided annually as guidance by the Office of the Under Secretary of Defense for Personnel & Readiness and conform to the prohibition of certain civilian personnel management constraints contained in 10 USC 129a.

[2] Retired military members can and do compete for appointment to SES positions. Thus, to a limited degree, positions requiring distinctly military competencies can be filled by SES members.

28

Depth and Breadth of Occupational Competencies

SES jobs tend to be found in areas where functional depth and continuity are valued. Because the total tenure of a military career is generally limited to about 35 years, including an average of only about 11 years at the GO level for those who reach O-10 in the Air Force, the job tenures of GOs tend to be relatively short, often one to two years. Additionally, many GOs have primary competencies in core warfighting occupations but, due to multifunctionality requirements, are holding jobs in areas of secondary competency. The Air Force has found it useful, in many cases, to arrange executive positions so that an SES member, with stability and depth in a function or organization, complements the relatively more mobile and more broadly experienced GOs moving through the same organization or function. As is depicted in Figure 4.1, functional expertise and position continuity can interact in various ways. The complementary SES and GO roles described here would fall in quadrants I and IV, respectively.

Not all SES jobs, however, place a heavy premium on stability and/or depth. Additionally, some mobility is required of SES members, particularly the more junior SES members, to develop them appropriately for the more senior SES positions. Thus, perhaps contrary to conventional expectations, we found that some SES jobs fall in quadrants II, III, or IV, depending on where they fit in a developmental career path and whether the broadening they are expected to impart to incumbents is across organizations (or organizational levels), functional areas, or both.

The premium placed on exceptional functional competence in many SES jobs is sometimes reflected in the narrower definitions of occupational competencies for SES positions relative to GO positions. The contrast can be seen in the two

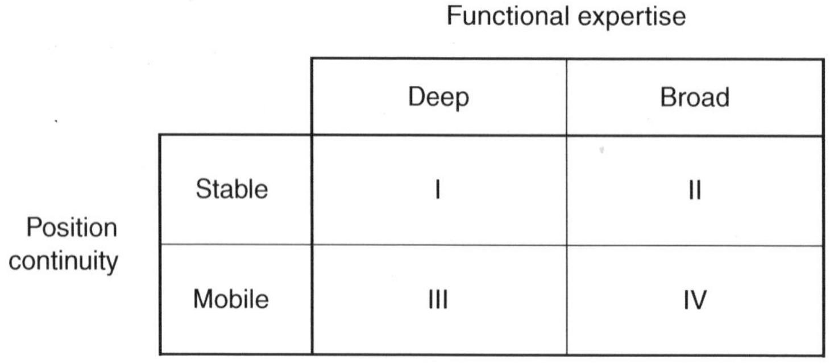

		Functional expertise	
		Deep	Broad
Position continuity	Stable	I	II
	Mobile	III	IV

RAND *TR175-4.1*

Figure 4.1—Combinations of Functional Expertise and Position Continuity Requirements

examples provided in Table 4.1. *Science and engineering* is considered a single occupational competency in our GO analysis but is divided into two more-specific competencies in our SES analysis. *Financial management*, a single competency in our GO analysis, is mapped to include four SES competencies.

Closely related to functional depth is the desirability, in some senior leader positions, for incumbents to possess doctoral degrees or other special qualifications, such as a certified public accountant (CPA) certification. These credentials are difficult for a member of the military to acquire, especially one on a career track leading to GO promotion. Senior leader positions with these requirements are most appropriately filled by members of the SES.

Senior Leader Grade Thresholds

Empirically, we discovered that our depiction of the correspondence between GO grades and SES tiers (see Figure 1.1, in Chapter One) was oversimplified in one respect: the thresholds between O-7 and SES tier 4 in the bottom layer of the senior leader pyramid and the military and civilian grades immediately below the pyramid (O-6 and GS-15, respectively) are shown as being perfectly aligned. GO positions in the Air Force are expected to be comparable in scope and responsibility to flag and GO positions in the other military services, whereas SES positions in the Air Force are expected to be comparable in scope and responsibility to SES positions throughout the federal government. For equity reasons, it is thus important for the O-6/O-7 threshold to remain aligned with that of the other services and for the GS-15/SES threshold to remain aligned with that of the other federal agencies. It is important to the Air Force that its O-6/O-7 threshold align with its GS-15/SES threshold, because the Air Force finds it

Table 4.1

Sample Comparisons of Selected GO and SES Competencies

GO Competencies	SES Competencies
Science and engineering	Laboratory science and engineering Product support engineering
Financial management	Accounting and finance Budget Cost and management analysis Auditing

useful to recognize and manage GOs and SES members in parallel ways. However, having that alignment be precise is less important than having these thresholds align with the external referents just mentioned. Our examination of the current sets of GO and SES jobs revealed that there are some SES positions, such as division chief positions on the Air Staff or department heads within a field organization, in which comparable military positions are generally filled by O-6s. However, we found no GO positions where a comparable civilian position was filled with an incumbent at grade GS-15.

Relaxing the Boundary

Notwithstanding the differences noted above, we concluded with Air Force decisionmakers that while some executive positions must be filled by GOs and some by SES members, others could be suitably filled by either a GO or an SES incumbent. Figure 4.2 depicts this overlapping pattern of SES and GO utilization.

To determine which positions fall into each of the three categories shown in Figure 4.2, we identified a series of logical filters and applied them to the Air Force's sets of current or (for joint positions) potential GO and SES positions. If one or more filters apply to a position, the job is suitable for GOs only or SES members only. If no filter applies, the job falls into the "either/or" category. Table 4.2 lists the filters.

Initially, PAF staff applied these filters to all career SES positions and all line GO positions. AFSLMO and a panel of GOs and senior SES members reviewed the results. Subsequently, as positions have been created and changed, PAF and AFSLMO staffs have reapplied the filters. In a recent compilation of GO and SES jobs, filters captured 77 percent of Air Force GO positions and all joint positions

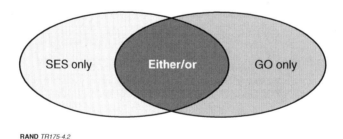

RAND *TR175-4.2*

Figure 4.2—Overlapping Suitability of SES and GO Utilization in Air Force Executive Positions

Table 4.2

Filters for Determining SES-Only and GO-Only Positions

Conditions for GO-Only Fill	Conditions for SES-Only Fill

Military occupation
  Position requires a military-only functional or occupational background
	Deep
	  Position requires functional depth not normally expected of GO incumbents

Command
  Position requires incumbent to exercise command of a military unit
	Stable
	  Position requires stability not normally expected of GO incumbents

Military discipline
  Position requires that incumbent exercise or be subject to the Uniform Code of Military Justice
	PhD/Certification
	  Position requires terminal academic degree or advanced certification not normally attainable in GO-producing career paths

Military experience
  Position requires military experience for credibility or similar reasons
	Civilian experience
	  Position requires civil service experience for credibility or other similar reasons

Joint military requirement
  Air Force does not have authority to switch position from GO to SES
	Joint civilian requirement
	  Air Force does not have authority to switch position from SES to GO

	O-6-equivalent position Comparable military positions are filled by O-6s

that Air Force GOs might fill, leaving 46 GO positions in the either/or category. Among career SES positions, filters caught 78 percent, leaving 34 in the either/or category. Depending on career progression needs and the availability of qualified candidates, AFSLMO (with appropriate concurrence from others) may either permanently switch some positions in this pool from GO to SES or vice-versa, or it may flexibly fill the positions by considering both GO and SES candidates whenever vacancies occur.

Benefits of a Flexible Boundary

Relaxing the GO/SES boundary provides AFSLMO with additional flexibilities for balancing the dual objectives of filling current positions with highly qualified senior leaders and developing senior leaders for greater responsibilities in the future. This is especially true in job pyramids that contain both GO and SES positions. Job qualifications and career development needs are unlikely to be in perfect balance within both GO and SES structures at all times. Flexibility in filling selected jobs allows the pattern of assignments to more easily capitalize on momentary strengths or to address momentary weaknesses in one or the other category.

Aided by the flow model described in Chapter Three, the Air Force can determine the proportion, over time, of GO and SES utilization in each either/or position that provides the best career progression pattern. In the following chapter, we describe how the flow model is used for analyses of this type. We also examine how relaxation of the GO/SES boundary permits AFSLMO new flexibilities in determining which positions will be filled by the Air Force's limited corps of senior leaders.

5. Objective Force Analysis

Like all military departments, the Air Force is limited in the number of GOs it may have in its ranks. Like all federal agencies, it is limited in the number of SES members it may have. And like most organizations, it usually finds that its demand for senior leader resources exceeds these limited supplies. AFSLMO periodically recommends to the Air Force senior leadership a way in which to allocate the limited supply of senior leaders across Air Force organizations and functions. The senior leader *objective force* is the subset of GO and SES jobs, taken from a larger set of actual or potential Air Force GO and SES jobs, that the Air Force, after meeting joint requirements, intends to fill on a continuing basis with GOs or SES members. In this chapter, we describe how occupational competency requirements and flow modeling can be used as part of an analytic method for determining the senior leader objective force.

In developing and revising the objective force, AFSLMO applies two considerations. First, it must place senior leaders in the organizations and the jobs within them where the need for maturity, judgment, skill, and accountability is the greatest. Second, it must ensure that the objective force contains career paths that can, at each grade or tier, develop qualified senior leaders and provide desired selectivity for the next higher grade or tier.

Because of the large number of positions involved and the complexity of the potential career paths through these positions, a purely intuitive approach to formulating the objective force is not likely to yield optimal results. Accordingly, AFSLMO asked PAF to develop a more rigorous method. That approach, as a first step, analyzes executive requirements across Air Force organizations (including functional staff elements) to determine at a very aggregate level (without respect to specific competencies) where the number of senior leaders might be high (over-supplied) or low (under-supplied) relative to other Air Force organizations. After choosing the least critical jobs in the potentially over-supplied organizations, this step yields a list of candidates for deletion from the objective force. Under-supplied organizations are identified in a similar fashion. In step 2, the flow model is presented with current job counts, any candidates for new jobs, any candidates for deletion identified in the first step, and lists of jobs in the GO/SES "either/or" pool. The flow model then identifies the subsets of GO and SES job counts that provide optimal career progression.

We now describe in detail these two steps of the approach that was developed, along with results obtained in an illustrative case.

Using an integrated approach to determine GO and SES objective forces provides AFSLMO with a powerful new set of flexibilities. When GO and SES objective forces are considered separately, introducing a new job into one of these two objective forces means that a job must also be deleted from that objective force. With an integrated approach, however (see Figure 5.1), the Air Force can depart from these conventional constraints. For example, if a new set of warfighting GO jobs had to be introduced, conventional considerations would demand that an equal number of lower-priority GO jobs be deleted or regraded. However, as indicated in Chapter Four, a number of SES jobs are equivalent to colonel positions and therefore quite possibly of lower priority than any GO job. The Air Force might prefer, if possible, to delete or regrade these or other lower-priority SES jobs in order to make room for the new warfighting GO jobs. It could do so by shifting an appropriate number of either/or positions from GO to SES. As a result of this sequence, the numbers of GO and SES jobs would remain constant, but the distribution of responsibility levels in jobs filled by SES members would be enriched.

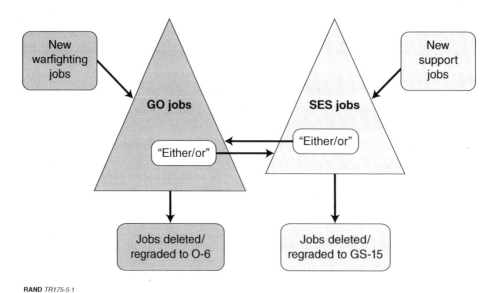

RAND *TR175-5.1*

Figure 5.1—Flexibilities in Determining the GO and SES Integrated Objective Force

Organizational Requirements for Senior Leaders

We did not attempt in our analysis to determine an *absolute* requirement for the total number of senior leaders within the Air Force. Rather, we limited our scope to determining the *relative* number of senior leaders required within each Air Force organization or staff element and whether the current distribution of senior leaders differed significantly from these relative needs.[1]

This analysis represents a departure from conventional reviews of senior leader position counts in that the unit of analysis is the *organization* rather than the individual *position*. In conventional reviews, individual positions are evaluated and prioritized using weighted criteria. In many cases, however, the characteristics attributed to individual positions are actually organizational characteristics. For example, the overall size of an organization's workforce might be considered a characteristic of the commander or director position and of other senior staff positions in the organization. We assumed that since organizational characteristics tend to dominate in senior leader position reviews, the appropriate unit of analysis is the organization rather than the individual position. Rather than rank-ordering individual positions, we sought to identify organizations whose numbers of executive positions seemed high or low compared with those of other organizations.

Theoretical Framework

The organizational literature suggests that the organizational characteristics most relevant to the required number of senior leaders are size and complexity. Size is reflected in many dimensions, including the volume of employees, revenue, expenditures, facilities, equipment, and product. As size increases, responsibility and accountability increase, implying that larger organizations require more executive leadership. But size is not the only driver of executive needs. Organizational complexity, defined as "the number of separate parts within an organization as reflected by the division of labor and by the number of both hierarchical levels and departments" is also relevant (Jablin, 1987, p. 400).

---

[1] Determining the absolute number of senior leaders required in an organization is a complex analytic task. It requires an understanding of factors such as internal and external compensation equity, the dynamics of up-or-out promotion systems and their effects on individual motivation and retention, and the scope, responsibility, and difficulty of each job—issues beyond the scope of this work.

Methodology

We distinguished organizations using a scheme that examines the clustering of senior leader positions. In the Air Force Secretariat and Air Staff, where there are multiple executive positions in each functional area, we found it useful to define each functional element (represented by a two-digit office symbol) as an organizational entity. For major commands (MAJCOMs) and below, where executive positions are often one-deep at the functional level, we defined the entire headquarters as a single organizational entity. All organizations down to wing level were included in the analysis.

We used multiple linear regression as the analysis procedure because it could provide insights about the set of organizational characteristics that jointly contribute to the need for executives. The general functional relationship for the regression analysis was:

$$\text{total executives} = F \text{ (organizational size, organizational level,} \\ \text{functional complexity)}$$

The dependent variable, total executives, counted the GOs, political appointees, and SES members executives in an organization's headquarters. The independent variables were defined as follows, using proxies available in the Air Force's Command Manpower Data Base (CMDB).[2]

Size. Organizational size was defined as the number of authorizations, including military, civilian, and contractor manpower equivalents, within a parent organization and all of its subordinate units.[3] Thus, for example, for each of the two-digit organizational entities in the Secretariat and Air Staff, we used the total number of authorizations in the Air Force.

Organizational Level. We defined six organizational levels: Secretariat, Air Staff, MAJCOM (or equivalent) headquarters, numbered air force (or equivalent) headquarters, center (or equivalent), wing (or equivalent), and other. Each level was represented as a dichotomous variable in the analysis.

Functional Complexity. The Air Force typically assigns functional management responsibilities in its organizations to colonels and civilians at the GS-15 pay grade. Accordingly, functional complexity was measured as the sum of colonel and GS-15 authorizations within the headquarters of each organization.

---

[2] For the analysis reported here, we used the CMDB as of the end of FY 2002.

[3] Given the wide variations found in organizational sizes, we used the logarithm of size in the regression analyses to obtain better results.

Our analysis recognized that the number of executive positions in an organization is related not only to the main effects variables (size, level, and functional complexity), but also to interactions among them. Thus, for example, the size variable can have a different effect at the Air Staff level than at the MAJCOM level. We examined a number of alternative regression models with varied interactions among the main effects variables, seeking a parsimonious model with a high correlation coefficient and favorable statistical properties.[4] The model that best fit these criteria contained three independent variables (log of size, organizational level, functional complexity) and one interaction variable (organizational level x functional complexity). The model's adjusted correlation coefficient, R^2, was 0.784. The F statistic indicated that the relationship was significant at the .0001 level. This is a very strong model: the three independent variables and the selected interactions among them predict with great confidence much of the variance in the numbers of executives across the organizations.

Identifying Outliers

Outlier organizations are those whose numbers of executives seem inconsistent with their size and complexity. Statistically, we were interested in organizations whose actual numbers of executives were outside of some confidence interval around the predicted number of executives. Since we were identifying jobs that were candidates for deletion (as offsets to permit the introduction of new, higher-priority executive positions elsewhere), we looked for outliers on the high side of the confidence interval.

For the illustrative case described here, AFSLMO asked us to introduce up to seven new warfighting GO positions into the objective force. In order to give the flow model some flexibility, we identified more than seven candidates for deletion. As Figure 5.2 indicates, we were able to identify, using a prediction interval with an 80 percent confidence level, seven organizations whose actual executive count fell above the interval.[5] The differences between the tops of the prediction intervals and the actual numbers of executive positions in these

---

[4] In a regression model, the multiple correlation coefficient (R^2) indicates the strength of the relationship between the dependent variable and the independent variables. Other statistical properties we considered were tests for homoskedasticity and for normality of the residuals.

[5] The *prediction interval* is calculated at some confidence level (*x* percent) so that x times out of a hundred the predicted value of the dependent variable for a case with the given values of the independent variable will lie within the computed prediction limits.

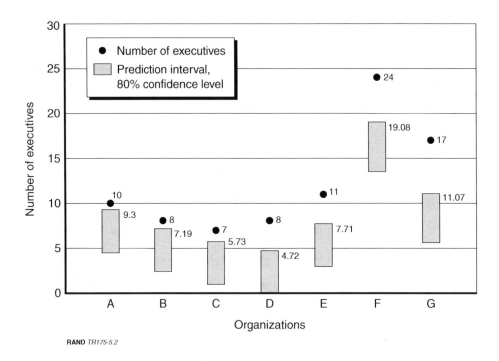

Figure 5.2—Outlier Organizations

organizations totaled 19.2. From these organizations, two GO and ten SES positions were identified as candidates for deletion.[6]

Career Progression Considerations

We adapted and merged the flow models described in Chapter 3 to help assess and guide changes in the mix of GO and SES jobs, aiming to improve the match between executives' occupational backgrounds and the jobs' competency requirements. The combined model can plan executive inventories, flows, and alignments that will fill the "either/or" jobs with GOs or SES members or a mix of the two over time. In effect, it recommends allocations of the either/or jobs between the GO and SES workforces.

The following job requirements information (by grade/tier, primary occupational competency, and secondary occupational competency) is fed into the model:

- Basic GO and SES job counts

_____

[6] Based on the analysis, up to 19 candidates could have been identified from the seven organizations depicted in figure 5.1. AFSLMO, applying additional considerations, selected only twelve candidates.

- Counts of any new GO and/or SES jobs

- Counts of either/or GO and SES jobs (identified as described in Chapter 4)

- Counts of candidates for deletion (identified as described above).

The model is allowed (or, if desired, can be forced) to bring in any or all new jobs, to realign any either/or jobs from GO to SES or vice-versa, and to delete an appropriate number of jobs from among the deletion candidates while it keeps the total number of GO and SES jobs in each grade/tier unchanged. Paralleling the separate GO and SES models, the integrated optimization's objective is to minimize the sum of the GO and SES total match quality scores. Beyond recommending incoming mixes of occupational backgrounds, promotion rates, and assignments for different categories of jobs at each grade/tier, the model's results tell how jobs could be rearranged to improve person-job match quality for both the GO and SES segments of the senior leader force.

In a typical run of this version of the flow model, we identified seven potential new GO warfighting jobs and twelve candidates for deletion (two GO and ten SES jobs). The model quantified the potential job shifts in various primary/secondary occupation combinations depicted by the arrows in Figure 5.1.

As a result of the job additions, deletions, and migrations, match quality improved. Table 5.1 shows the average and distributions of match quality *before* and *after* the combined optimization. For example, before job additions, deletions, or migrations were allowed, the average match quality in the GO model was 1.39, with 230.9 jobs at match quality 1, 12.9 jobs at match quality 2, and so on. After job shifts were allowed, the count of jobs at match quality 1 increased to 235.7, and the average match quality improved to 1.35. More-dramatic improvements can be noted in the SES data.

Table 5.1

Match Quality Before and After Job Additions, Deletions, and Migrations

Match Quality	GO		SES	
	Before	After	Before	After
Average match quality	1.39	1.35	2.01	1.64
Count at match quality 1	230.9	235.7	75.7	104.0
Count at match quality 2	12.9	10.6	30.7	18.8
Count at match quality 3	4.6	3.3	8.3	3.3
Count at match quality 4	21.9	21.5	24.9	11.4
Count at match quality 5	4.7	3.8	6.4	8.5

6. A Decision Support System to Facilitate Utilization and Development of Senior Leaders

The job competency database and GO and SES flow models provide an analytic basis for planning the Air Force's executive workforce. If married to information on the current competencies of GOs and SES members, these tools could be adapted to aid in the day-to-day management of senior leader resources. This chapter describes the Succession Analysis and Planning Assistant (SAPA), a prototype system that we constructed to illustrate one way to use our planning tools to address day-to-day management concerns.

In developing SAPA, we had to contend with certain complexities and limitations inherent in the planning tools:

- First, no single solution from the flow model is uniquely *right*. Many solutions reflect the same overall quality of match. The Air Force would be mistaken to try to align the senior leader force, both GO and SES, to just one solution. Management activities should be performed with the understanding that a range of management actions can produce acceptable management solutions.

- Second, the flow models manipulate *notional* executive workforces. Model solutions are structured to maximize match quality while assuring acceptable promotion and assignment selectivities. Because they focus only on primary/secondary occupational competencies and do not include other leadership attributes (e.g., functional familiarities, cross-functional competencies, date of rank, date assigned to current position), these solutions present only part of the plan for managing real-world GO and SES members. Sometimes these additional attributes may be more important than primary/secondary occupational competencies in determining assignments.

- Finally, the flow models represent a steady-state or temporally consistent environment, reflecting the same numbers of promotions and retirements from each primary/secondary occupational competency pair within each grade during *every* year. The real world, of course, is not so consistent. Numbers of promotions vary annually, driven directly by numbers of retirements. One challenge in executive workforce management is to structure annual actions (e.g., promotions and assignments) so as to anticipate the effects of these *peaks and valleys* in the executive inventory. Care must be taken not to overreact in any one year to unusually large or unusually small numbers of retirements or promotions of leaders with given backgrounds, and to try to keep the averages over time fairly close to values identified using the planning models.

The SAPA prototype demonstrates how to deal with these complexities and limitations in the context of one of AFSLMO's most prominent day-to-day management processes: providing assignment candidate rosters for each assignment decision. The rosters address both immediate tactical and future strategic issues, aiming to help maximize the size of candidate rosters in the future *(assignment selectivity)*, the predicted effectiveness of candidates' performance *(match quality)* in both the near and the long term, and movement toward the desired integrated objective force. SAPA can help succession managers cope with the complex simultaneity of these interacting goals.

In the parlance of senior leader succession planning, these candidate rosters are referred to as *daisy chains*. A daisy chain is a set of related promotion, assignment, and retirement events, including one such initial event. Every other event in the chain depends directly or indirectly on the initial event. For example, the initial event could be someone's retirement, and all other events in the set could then correspond to filling the vacancy created by the retirement or backfilling vacancies created by previous assignments in the chain.

Decision support systems (DSSs) help decisionmakers overcome known limitations of human cognition, especially with respect to managing complexity and coping with large decision spaces. Examples of complexity inherent in the succession-management domain include

- Interactions that are intricate and intertwined
- Large amounts of data to comprehend simultaneously
- Many dependencies, such as potential position assignment ramifications.

DSSs help with the complexity of domains such as succession management by making it easier for decisionmakers to navigate and visualize the problem's data space. A DSS can provide the *big picture* overview and a convenient way to drill down to details more effectively than reports, spreadsheets, and database queries can. Furthermore, such systems allow decisionmakers to focus on a *local neighborhood* while ensuring that global issues are simultaneously being considered.

The essential capabilities of a fully functional SAPA were identified through meetings and interviews with AFSLMO personnel in which requirements for both SES and GO management were considered. These capabilities would include

- **Support assignment functions.** Support today's assignment process—i.e., help AFSLMO make the best assignments today—and support the planning needed to develop senior leaders for future assignments. For example, assignment decisions today should improve future selectivity and career path potentials while at the same time achieving an acceptable level of current effectiveness.[1] Assignment functions are specific examples of the complex interactions that require DSS support, since they can have many conditional and simultaneous interactions.

- **Support promotion planning.** Help AFSLMO personnel formulate GO promotion guidance, informed by aggregate promotion and tenure objectives.

- **Support integrated objective force planning.** Assess how assignment decisions would affect the objective force now and in the future.

- **Improve access to interrelated data.** Help decisionmakers navigate the problem's data space and explore the solution space. Typical requests include hypotheticals (*What if?*) and explanations (*Why?*). Support access to interrelated data not currently accessible through queries to individual databases or files.

As indicated above, the SAPA prototype addressed only the first of these capabilities, and only one aspect of that capability. The intent of the prototype was to assess the feasibility of developing such a system, integrating leading-edge computer science, software engineering, and policy analysis. The prototype was built using best practices for maintainable, field-viable software in order that the outcomes would provide data and guidance that AFSLMO could use to evaluate the costs and benefits of further exploration and development. Ongoing development of a data support system product exceeds the normal scope of PAF's charter. Accordingly, PAF and AFSLMO agreed that the research and exploratory aspects were within PAF's purview but that product development would remain outside the scope of PAF support.

---

[1] Like the position requirements database and optimization solutions, the executive inventory is couched in terms of primary and secondary occupational competencies.

Support for GO Assignment Cycles

The Air Force moves almost half its GOs to new assignments annually, reflecting an average time on assignment of about two years. These moves take place for two reasons: officers must be moved to fill vacancies when other GOs are promoted or retire, and officers need to be moved for development purposes—i.e., to let them develop and/or demonstrate skills they will need to fill future, more senior assignments.

During any given year, from 30 to 60 GOs may retire, with the average being about 40. Retirements are generally known well enough in advance to permit reasonable assignment planning (e.g., an officer who is going to reach his/her mandatory retirement date in the coming year is going to leave a vacancy). If the retiring officer has a high grade, the impact on assignments will be greater than if he/she has a lower grade. For example, a retiring lieutenant general will leave a vacancy that must be filled by either another lieutenant general or by a major general selected for promotion to lieutenant general. This is called a *primary* vacancy. The vacancy that results from filling the primary vacancy, called a *secondary* vacancy, must also be filled, and the vacancy resulting from that assignment, also a secondary vacancy, must be filled as well. The GO daisy chain ends when a brigadier general selectee fills a secondary vacancy or an assignment creates no secondary vacancy (e.g., when an officer returns from a joint assignment whose next incumbent will be from another service). A given higher-grade retirement may result in ten or more secondary vacancies, and a primary major general vacancy can result in three or more secondary vacancies.

SAPA is designed to help AFSLMO staff work the GO assignment process. It enables direct and immediate access to person and position data; detailed information about the person currently assigned to a position is accessible as a searchable personnel brief (i.e., a specifically formatted display of current and historical information about a specific person). If a position is a primary vacancy-generating position, SAPA allows one or more consistent daisy chain excursions to be created.

For the primary vacancy and each subsequent secondary vacancy, SAPA identifies a candidate pool for the position. Each candidate pool is selected using a DSS-specific fillmap, modeled after GO and SES flow model fillmaps. The DSS-specific fillmap currently has seven levels of match quality, two more than the flow model fillmaps. The additional levels are necessary because officers in AFSLMO databases may lack targeted primary or secondary occupational competencies. The DSS-specific fillmap can be expanded and enhanced to include match quality for measures such as functional familiarity and cross-functional competency. It is used to compute a measure representing the quality of an overall mapping of persons to positions, the so-called organizational model (OM) state score, or OM score.[2]

Persons in the candidate pool are initially rank-ordered by their DSS-specific match quality to the open position, the best matches appearing first. Additional person attributes are immediately available to AFSLMO decisionmakers for each person in the candidate pool (e.g., primary/secondary competencies, date of rank, date assigned to current position, and mandatory retirement date). The personnel brief for any person in the candidate pool may also be accessed, providing further candidate attribute details for AFSLMO decisionmakers to consider. The impact of choosing a specific person from the candidate pool to fill the vacancy is immediately displayed as an adjustment to the OM score.

The AFSLMO analyst can develop alternative parallel daisy chains for either a primary or a secondary vacancy, each alternative having different candidates filling the vacancies. This process, called cloning, allows the analyst to take a partial daisy chain solution and explore alternative completions for it from that cloning point. In all cases, persons previously selected to fill vacancies are specially highlighted in the candidate pool to prevent inconsistent solutions (i.e., daisy chains in which an officer appears more than once) from being created. The daisy chain solutions preferred by the AFSLMO analyst can be saved to disk for later retrieval and processing.

The SAPA prototype has demonstrated that AFSLMO can derive significant benefits from a DSS. Ongoing use of the DSS depends on the availability of accurate and up-to-date data.

---

[2] The DSS reflects jobs arranged in a multilevel hierarchy called the organization model. An assignment of persons to jobs in the hierarchical organization is thus called an OM state. A vector of measures indicating the appropriateness and desirability of an OM state is called an OM score.

7. Conclusions and Recommendations

In this chapter, we summarize our conclusions regarding the use of the competency framework and database, flow model, and other related tools to enhance the management of senior leaders. We also provide recommendations on how our tools and methods can be usefully extended.

Multifunctionality Is Needed

While many current officers and civil service employees have pursued career development within stovepipes, where the bulk of their career is spent within a single functional area, the research reported here suggests that most senior leaders need to be expert in multiple occupational competencies. On the *demand* side—i.e., when considering the occupational competency requirements of jobs, we learned that many jobs are better performed if the incumbents have multiple (primary and secondary) functional backgrounds. Further, the positions associated with some occupational competencies are top heavy in that there are more high-grade than low-grade positions, whereas the positions associated with other competencies are bottom heavy, or have an hourglass shape, or even have missing intermediate grades. Finally, many positions can be filled acceptably (but at a lower match quality) with officers who meet some but not all of the primary/secondary requirements, and other positions can be filled acceptably with officers who have more-general primary competencies (e.g., a rated officer as opposed to a fighter pilot) and more-general secondary competencies (e.g., an officer with *any* secondary competency).

On the *supply* side, in a closed personnel system, positions in variously shaped occupational competency pyramids have to be filled by moving individuals among those pyramids. To minimize the placing of senior leaders in positions for which they lack the necessary experience, individuals must gain experience in more than one functional area prior to reaching the senior grades. The job competency requirements database and flow model permit a systematic examination of how supply should be allocated to meet demand. Through an optimization process, and guided by sensible force-shaping constraints, the model simultaneously evaluates multiple assignment tradeoffs and creates notional inventories that both maximize the overall quality of inventory-to-job matching and assure acceptable promotion and assignment selectivity. These notional inventories form templates for developing pools of highly competitive officers and civil service employees from which to choose future senior leaders. When given flexibility, the flow model also permits one to examine how demand should be adjusted simultaneously with supply to improve the overall demand/supply match.

The Tools Can Be Used to Evaluate Current and Expected Outcomes

Flow model results provide a variety of benchmarks for assessing the competencies available among both current and future inventories of senior leaders.

Assessing the Current Senior Leader Inventory

Virtual inventory templates generated using the flow model can help the Air Force identify critical primary/secondary occupational competency areas where inventory is insufficient to assure acceptable promotion and assignment selectivity, and where inventory is in surplus. In working assignment actions, the areas with surplus inventory can provide candidates for broadening into assignments that qualify individuals for higher-level assignments in the deficient areas.

Assessing Promotion Board Results

In addition to providing primary/secondary competency templates for the inventory in each grade, the flow model provides primary/secondary occupational competency templates for promotions into each grade. This capability could be used to inform or guide promotion board selections. Alternatively, as is the preferred course in the Air Force, it can serve as the basis for assessing the results of promotion boards.[1] Are the boards, for example, selecting officers with acceptable primary/secondary competencies to meet GO requirements? If not, where are the deficiencies and surpluses? Knowing where deficiencies and surpluses exist can also inform assignment decisions.

---

[1] The Air Force prefers that its promotion boards select the best-qualified candidates without regard to occupational competencies. It seeks to get an appropriate distribution of occupational competencies in its brigadier general selectees by developing appropriate distributions of competencies within the pools of highly competitive colonels being considered for promotion.

Assessing Career Development Patterns

The template for promotion to grade O-7 or SES is especially important for guiding the career development of field-grade officers and middle-grade civil service employees who are expected to be competitive for future senior leader selections. Emerging patterns of multifunctionality among these developing cohorts can be compared to the templates for O-7 and SES entry cohorts. Critical deficiencies can be addressed by deliberately assigning competitive individuals to positions that develop required secondary occupational competencies.

The Tools Can Be Used to Evaluate Demand

During the study, it became apparent that the flow model, originally devised specifically to determine development templates, could also help optimize the mix of GO and SES jobs in the senior leader objective force. When married to an approach for evaluating the distribution of senior leaders across organizations and allowed to take advantage of the flexibilities afforded by a prudently relaxed GO/SES boundary, the flow model can help the Air Force formulate objective forces that optimize *utilization* of senior leaders.

The Tools Can Be Further Enhanced

Two forces drive the flow model's continued development. First, we recognize some fundamental limitations in the model's structure and seek ways to reduce or eliminate them. Second, AFSLMO continually identifies management issues for which the flow model and other ancillary tools developed in this study can be used to evaluate options. Some potential enhancements driven by these forces are as follows.

First, we see potential gain in adding *learning* to the model. The flow model currently does not expand a virtual individual's set of primary/secondary skills as a result of that individual's having held a senior leader position. The skills with which virtual inventories enter the senior leader ranks remain unchanged as the inventories progress through the various GO grades or SES tiers. We want to enhance the model so that holding a position with specific primary/secondary competency requirements also gives the virtual inventory a recognized additional competency. With this capability, we can envision one or more optimization steps that try to steer broadening in the direction of short-supply skills.

Second, we see potential gain in adding tiered assignments within a GO grade to the model.[2] While the model currently considers specific assignments (at least in terms of primary/secondary competencies), it does not identify which assignments should be held as a first assignment in a grade, as a second, or as either a first or a second. By providing for tiered assignments, the model will treat assignment selectivities more explicitly, will perhaps reveal additional serial multifunctionality requirements, and will have more flexibility in sensing the need to employ learning to broaden officers in desired competency directions.

Third, we see benefits in extending the model to encompass grades O-6 and GS-15. These grades are included in AFSLMO's workforce management responsibilities. Development of more junior officers and employees to fill needs at these grades may be of less relative importance than development aimed at filling senior leader jobs, but it is nonetheless important. Work has already been done to capture and review occupational requirements for O-6 positions, including their tiering. Development of the model to incorporate these requirements could reveal important multifunctionality needs among cohorts competing for promotion to O-6 and GS-15.

Fourth, and related to the tiered assignment enhancement, we see potential benefits in converting the model from an aggregate perspective (expressing requirements and virtual inventory in terms of primary/secondary occupational competency pairs) to a detailed, job-level and individual person-level perspective (making it an *entity* model, in the vernacular of simulation modeling). This would allow more fidelity in many aspects of the model.

The Tools Have Value in Other Contexts

The methods and tools described in this document have proven to be of great value to the Air Force. They have enabled a competency-based, requirements-driven senior leader development approach—the basis for a force development doctrine that is transforming how the Air Force prepares its most promising mid-grade officers and civilians to eventually assume GO and SES responsibilities. It has also led to a rethinking of traditional GO and SES boundaries—the basis for merging the separate offices that formerly managed GO and SES resources.

Other organizations with relatively closed personnel systems could benefit from the methods described here in formulating templates for optimal development of

---

[2] We do not anticipate further subdivision of the SES tiers. The current tier structure was devised with an anticipation that there would be very limited movement between jobs within the same tier.

experience-based human capital. Organizations with bifurcated workforces—such as the State Department with its foreign service and non-foreign service components, and the Federal Bureau of Investigation with its law enforcement and non-law enforcement components—could benefit from using the methods described here to examine the boundaries between these components in their senior leadership forces. Leadership does make a difference in organizations. There is every reason to believe that more deliberately developed leadership will improve organizational performance.

Appendix

A. Job Characteristics and Factors in the GO Survey

Table A.1 lists GO job characteristics ascertained through the GO survey. Where applicable, the table also indicates which characteristics loaded against the eleven factors identified in the factor analysis described in Chapter Two. (An x in a factor column indicates that the characteristic loads against that factor.) The first two groups of job characteristics—functional area and aircraft/weapon system operations—were the basis for developing primary and secondary occupational competencies and familiarities and were not included in the factor analysis. The remaining job characteristics were included in the factor analysis, forming the basis for cross-functional competencies.

Table A.1

GO Job Characteristics and Their Factor Loadings

Factor Loadings. Factors I–XI are: I = Management; II = Operational Awareness; III = Analytic Skill; IV = Geopolitical Awareness; V = Resource Management; VI = Communication Skill; VII = Policy and Planning; VIII = Command and Headquarters Experience; IX = Civilian Management; X = Non-DoD Agency Awareness; XI = Space Operational Awareness.

Job Characteristics	I	II	III	IV	V	VI	VII	VIII	IX	X	XI
FunctionalArea											
Air power employment											
Space employment											
Missile employment (ICBM)											
Education/training											
R&D											
Test & evaluation											
C2ISR											
Communications											
Intelligence											
Civil engineering											
Force protection											
IT or electronics											
Financial management											
IG											
Contracting											
Logistics											
Safety											
Personnel/manpower											
Acquisition											
Political military/ security assistance											
Other											
Aircraft/Weapon-System Operatons											
Airlift											
Bomber											
Exp/Test											
Fighter											
Helicopter											
Trainer											
Recon/surv/electr warfare/air battle manager											
Tanker											
Other											
Operational Knowledge											
Information		X									X
Special operations		X		X							X
Nuclear		X									
Missile											X
Space		X									X
Conventional air		X									
Other											
Operational Credibility		X									
Theater Environment											
Africa				X							
Asia		X		X							
Europe/Russia		X		X							
Middle East		X		X							
South America				X							
Other											
One of the above											
General background											
Foreign language		X		X							

Table A.1—continued

Job Characteristics	I Management	II Operational Awareness	III Analytic Skill	IV Geopolitical Awareness	V Resource Management	VI Communication Skill	VII Policy and Planning	VIII Command and Headquarters Experience	IX Civilian Management	X Non-DoD Agency Awareness	XI Space Operational Awareness
AF/DoD/GOV'T Systems/Processes											
Non-DOD Agencies			X		X					X	X
Joint Issues											
Joint operations		X									
Joint doctrine		X									
Joint weapon systems		X	X								
Combined operations		X									
Other											
Operations & Planning											
Strategic		X					X				
AF doctrine		X					X				
AF weapons, tactics		X									
Deliberate/crisis planning		X									
Operations above wing level		X					X				
Other											
Resource Management			X								
PPBS					X						
Planning					X						
Programming					X						
Budgeting					X						
Execution					X				X		
Other											
Reserve/Guard		X					X				
Requirements		X	X								
Manage Civilians											
Employees	X								X		
Contractors			X						X		
Prior Jobs											
Wing commander		X									X
Operations group cmdr		X									
Support group cmdr								X			
Logistics group cmdr								X			
Any group commander							X				
Squadron or above cmdr								X			
Tour in like command											
Tour in region		X									
MAJCOM HQ tour								X			
OSD Pentagon								X			X
Joint Staff Pentagon								X			
HAF Pentagon			X				X				
Any Pentagon											
Other											
Education											
Science/engineering			X								
Social science		X	X				X				
At least one											
Other											

Table A.1—continued

Job Characteristics	I Management	II Operational Awareness	III Analytic Skill	IV Geopolitical Awareness	V Resource Management	VI Communication Skill	VII Policy and Planning	VIII Command and Headquarters Experience	IX Civilian Management	X Non-DoD Agency Awareness	XI Space Operational Awareness
Comunication											
Good/Bad News Skill											
Internal to AF	X					X					
Other DoD agencies			X			X					
Non-DoD agencies						X					
Congress						X					
General public						X			X		
Negotiation Skills											
Tact/diplomacy	X	X							X		
Negotiator	X										
Political sensitivity	X					X					
Academic/Technical											
Qualitative/Analytic											
Using model results			X								
Analysis			X								
Detail orientation			X								
Search/integrate info			X								
Other											
Develop/Evaluate AF Policy							X				
Management											
Activities											
Planning	X						X		X		
Organization	X										
System development	X		X								
Prioritizing	X										
Change agent	X										
Implementation	X										
Interpersonal Skill											
Coordination	X										
Relate to non-military	X										
Teamwork	X										
Customer relations	X										
Public relations	X						X				
Other											
Abilities											
Visionary	X										
Creative	X										
Complexities	X										
Analytic	X										
Abstract problems	X						X				
Concentration	X										
People perspective	X								X		
Warfighting Perspective	X	X									

B. Flow Model Specifications

The flow models used in the analysis are implemented with the General Algebraic Modeling System (GAMS) language, linked to an appropriate solver. GAMS facilitates the use of mathematical programming by allowing analysts to efficiently represent algebraic relationships in these flow models. The flow models' algebraic specifications are compiled by GAMS, resulting in model specifications specifically prepared for the solver chosen for use by the analyst. GAMS also provides facilities for reading and processing the solution generated by the selected solver. GAMS and the solver provide additional reporting and diagnostic features.

A linear programming model optimizes one or more *objective functions* composed of *decision variables*, subject to a set of *constraints*. Both the objective functions and the constraints are expressed as linear equations.

GAMS models have only one objective function, but multi-objective programming problems can be solved in GAMS either by using a linear weighted cost function of the multiple objectives or through lexicographic model definition. We used the lexicographic model definition approach. In that approach the dominance of each objective function is clearly defined, and single objective solutions are ordered according to dominance. An additional constraint is added to each dominated model to constrain its solution to previous dominating objectives' solutions.

Linear programs are usually specified according to strict conventions for the forms of the objective functions and constraints (e.g., standard, canonical, and mixed forms). GAMS allows the analyst to more flexibly specify equations in forms that are readable to the analyst.

GAMS also allows indexing, or subscripting, of expressions, so that GAMS may use a single GAMS equation to generate hundreds or thousands of constraints. GAMS extends and formats the equations, constructing the strict form required by the selected solver during the compilation phase.

In the following sections of this appendix, simplified versions of actual GAMS expressions are used to provide the essential elements of the model. These elements consist of parameters, variables, sets, and equations. The conventions we use here are that parameters are in uppercase text, variables are in lowercase, and sets are italicized.

A parameter is a symbol representing a value provided as input to the model. The important parameters are REQUIREMENTS (counts of the numbers of jobs in each combination of primary competency, secondary competency, and grade/tier), FILLMAP (the match quality for a given job-to-personnel type match), PROMOTION RATE (annual rate of promotion/advancement from one grade or tier to the next), PROMOTION FLEX (allowable promotion flexibility), and TIME IN GRADE (duration before promotion or retirement in a given grade).

A variable is a symbol representing a value to be determined by the model. The important variables are inventory (the number of each personnel type in the model solution), assignment (the quantity of a specific REQUIREMENT type that is filled by a specific personnel type), and quality score (the sum of match qualities across all assignments).

A set is an index used to differentiate within a collection of like parameters or variables; it performs the function of a subscript in formal mathematical notation. The key sets used in the flow model are *primjob* (primary occupational competencies and bins applicable to the set of jobs being analyzed), *secjob* (secondary occupational competencies and bins applicable to the set of jobs being analyzed), *priminv* (primary occupational competencies to be represented in the virtual inventory), *secinv* (secondary occupational competencies to be represented in the virtual inventory), and *grade* (the four GO grades) or *tier* (the four SES tiers). In GAMS, sets are shown within parentheses following a parameter, a variable, or an operator such as "sum".

An equation expresses mathematical relationships among parameters and variables. To preserve linearity in the model, relationships among variables must be additive—equations containing powers or roots of variables, products of variables, or division of one variable by another are not allowed.

Actual GAMS specifications are simplified in the following expressions in several ways. First, GAMS requires equations and other expressions to be labeled. We have omitted the labeling. Second, to preclude the generation of unneeded constraints, GAMS allows for notation that indicates which members of a set should be skipped in an indexed operation. We have omitted these notations. Third, although the GO and SES versions of the model involve some differences in technique or labeling, we use GO flow model examples here as the foundation for the following simplified expressions. Finally, in the interest of depicting the essential form of the model, we have omitted many of the more nuanced relationships reflected in the full model.

Objective Function

In the basic versions of the flow models, the objective function seeks to minimize the sum of match qualities across all jobs.[1] The simplified GAMS specification for this sum is

(1) overall quality score =

$$\text{sum}((primjob, secjob, priminv, secinv, grade),$$
$$\text{assignment } (primjob, secjob, priminv, secinv, grade) *$$
$$\text{FILLMAP } (primjob, secjob, priminv, secinv))$$

This is equivalent to the following standard mathematical expression, where q = overall quality score, a = assignment, F = specific quality score from the fillmap, and subscripts $i = primjob$, $j = secjob$, $k = priminv$, $l = secinv$, and $m = grade$:

$$q = \sum_{i,j,k,l,m} \left(a_{i,j,k,l,m} \cdot F_{i,j,k,l} \right)$$

Constraints

The assignment variable serves as a link between the REQUIREMENTS parameter and the inventory variable. It indicates how much of each inventory type (described by primary occupation, secondary occupation, and grade) is assigned to each REQUIREMENT (also described by primary occupation, secondary occupation, and grade). Assignments summed across inventory types must equal REQUIREMENTS, while assignments summed across REQUIREMENTS must equal inventories. The two simplified GAMS specifications that express this relationship are

(2) REQUIREMENTS((primjob, secjob, grade) =

$$\text{sum}((priminv, secinv), \text{assignment } (primjob, secjob, priminv,$$
$$secinv, grade))$$

---

[1] In the formulation below, all assignments are treated equally, irrespective of GO grade or SES tier. In some model formulations, higher weights are assigned to higher grades/tiers. In other cases, higher weights are assigned to poorer match qualities. In any of these cases, higher weights increase the penalties for poorer matches.

(3) inventory (*priminv, secinv, grade*) =

$$\text{sum}((\textit{primjob, secjob}), \text{assignment} (\textit{primjob, secjob, priminv, secinv, grade}))$$

Little's Theorem (see Chapter Three) is reflected in the relationship between inventory, PROMOTION RATE, and TIME IN GRADE, as expressed in the following simplified GAMS specification:

(4) inventory (*priminv, secinv, grade*) ≤

$$\text{inventory} (\textit{priminv, secinv, grade} - 1) * \text{PROMOTION}$$
$$\text{RATE} (\textit{grade}) * \text{PROMOTION FLEX} (\textit{priminv}) *$$
$$\text{TIME IN GRADE} (\textit{grade})$$

Since the simplified GAMS specification (4) allows some flexibility across occupational competencies (implemented as the PROMOTION FLEX parameter), a constraint is needed to ensure that the total inventory in each *grade* equals the total REQUIREMENTS in each *grade*. The simplified GAMS specification that enforces this relationship is

(5) sum ((*priminv, secinv*), inventory (*priminv, secinv, grade*)) =

$$\text{sum} ((\textit{primjob, secjob}), \text{REQUIREMENTS}$$
$$(\textit{primjob, secjob, grade}))$$

One of the fundamental considerations in this study was providing minimally acceptable promotion and assignment selectivity whenever possible. Promotion selectivity is assured by the following equation, in which the promotion selectivity factor, PROMOTION SELECTIVITY, is typically set equal to three. In selected primary/secondary occupational combinations, however, this constraint must be relaxed in order to generate a feasible solution. The time in grade parameters in this constraint serve to limit the inventory appearing in the first term of the equation to those eligible for promotion to the next higher grade. A similar but more complex constraint is used in the GO model to constrain inventories so as to obtain minimum job selectivity whenever possible.

(6) inventory (*priminv, secinv, grade* – 1) *

$$((\text{TIME IN GRADE} (\textit{grade} - 1) -$$
$$\text{MIN TIME IN GRADE} (\textit{grade} - 1) /$$
$$\text{TIME IN GRADE} (\textit{grade} - 1)) \geq$$
$$\text{PROMOTION SELECTIVITY} (\textit{priminv, secinv,}$$
$$\textit{grade}) *$$
$$\text{promotions} (\textit{priminv, secinv, grade})$$

References

Harvey, R. J. (1991). "Job Analysis," in M. D. Dunnette and L. M. Hough (eds.), *Handbook of Industrial and Organizational Psychology: Volume 2.* Palo Alto, CA: Consulting Psychologists Press, Inc. (pp. 71–163).

Ilgen, D. R., and J. R. Hollenbeck (1991). "The Structure of Work: Job Design and Roles," in M. D. Dunnette and L. M. Hough (eds.), *Handbook of Industrial and Organizational Psychology: Volume 2.* Palo Alto, CA: Consulting Psychologists Press, Inc. (pp. 165–207).

Jablin, F. M. (1987). "Formal Organizational Structure," in F. M. Jablin, L. L. Putnam, K. H. Roberts, and L. W. Porter (eds.), *Handbook of Organizational Communication.* Newbury Park, CA: Sage Publications.

Little, John D.C. (1961). "A Proof of the Queuing Formula: L= λW," *Operations Research*, Vol. 9, May, pp. 383–387.

Morrison, Robert F., and Roger R. Hock (1986). "Career Building: Learning from Cumulative Work Experience," in Douglas T. Hall (ed.), *Career Development in Organizations.* New Jersey: Jossey-Bass.

Nunnally, J. C. (1978). *Psychometric Theory* (2nd ed.). New York: McGraw-Hill.

Ward, J. H. (1963). "Hierarchical Grouping to Optimize an Objective Function," *Journal of the American Statistical Association*, Vol. 58, pp. 236–244.